AF269243

FIND YOUR SONG
Last Leaves from a Diversity of Trees

Love and Lost Love Lyrics
Country Western Epics and Ballads
Cowboy Tales and Appalachian Opera
Hallelujahs, Drinkin' and Go, USA!
Funny Stuff and other Stuff
…& Shakespeare too!

Robert Emmett McGill

A publication of Self-Knowledge College Press

ISBN: 978-1-988277-22-6

SKC Press
356 Westridge Drive, Waterloo, Ontario, N2L 5Y3
226-674-6961

Inquiries: daleyfrank0@gmail.com

Contact the author: rmcgill7@att.net

May You Find Your Song

Robert E. McGill

FOR

KATHLEEN ANN McGILL

My Sister, My Savior, My Best Friend

*AE*DH WISHES FOR THE CLOTHS OF HEAVEN

Had I the heavens' embroidered cloths,
Enwrought with golden and silver light,
The blue and the dim and the dark cloths
Of night and light and the half light,
I would spread the cloths under your feet:
But I, being poor, have only my dreams;
I have spread my dreams under your feet;
Tread softly because you tread on my dreams.

Yeats, W. B. 1865 – 193

TABLE OF CONTENTS

CHAPTER 1:

**COWBOY POETRY, BALLADS
AND CAMPFIRE TALES.**

I'm Cookie, though my real name is known to very few. My real first name is "Hoo," or "Hoot" or – like when you sit down on a nail - "Whahoo!" What's that about? I wish I knew. I must have scared my mother half to death; or the owl cried – that's what I'd like to think. Why else would you call a baby, Hoo?" Maybe some distant relative I never knew. I never got to ask my Mom. She died when I was two.

So, you can call me Cookie. That's what the crew all do. I'm in charge of feeding all my boys: And that's what they all are. Each and every one is – old or young – each and every one: my son. I'm the only one they can all talk too. I look away, avert my eyes, when one of them sits beside me and cries a bit; when he talks about his girl, or his mother or his fears that the other guys don't respect him. What they all realize is, I'm not gonna tell a soul, whatever they confess.

And so: It's mid 1870's, Chisolm trail: fifteen hundred miles long and a hundred miles wide. We're driving three thousand head of cattle, north to Kansas City, resting for a moment, this afternoon, while the herd drinks at the river. A late-middle age Cowboy approaches.

HEY, COOKIE

Robert E. McGill

Hey, Cookie. I'm leaving you some spices
That my Mom snuck in my bed-roll years ago.
Now, no complaint intended; but as nice as
Your stews and chilis are, you ought to know

I'll be riding out sometime, later this evenin'.
I've told the trail boss. He says it's alright.
If I never used these spices, Mom'd be grievin,'
So, can you cook them for the boys and me tonight?

Don't know if you're a reader, Bill;
But I've a book for you.
You'll understand the words are grand;
But all of them are true.
Best thing, the author has the same first name as you.

We're just a half-day's drive from Kansas City:
Baths and booze and women by our side.
Pick the lady of light virtue I would: sweet and pretty.
I've got one last round-up I must ride.

I'm gonna find a place I know.
Best place I'll ever be.
Once there, I'll let my Pinto go.
If he makes it back, you take care of him for me?

I've got a bad ache, William; there's no cure.
I did the best I could. I have no fear.
"But this rough magic, I here abjure." [i]
Hey, Cookie, get those spices right, you hear?

----

[i] Shakespeare, William. THE TEMPEST. Prospero, Act 5, scene 1

STOCKYARD LULLABY

Robert E. McGill

Go to sleep, my little dogies, go to sleep.
The Lord above will guard you through the night.
Go to sleep, my little dogies, go to sleep.
I'm here too. I'll care for you. Everything's alright.

You're restless, little dogies. Are you aware
Why we've slowed down the last few days or so;
Why we've let you eat to put on extra meat?
Is that's what bothrin' you, or do you care?

Do you smell death lurking, smirking in the air?
We made you march a thousand miles to die. (*Spoken*) Hell, that ain't fair.
Your journey's done; your travel and travail.
K.C. tomorrow. Then Chicago. End of the trail.

> We're men driving cattle;
> But we're also driven men.
> Knowing where we're going;
> Knowing where we've been;
> But the purpose of it all?
> Well, that's the real question.

If you knew what was awaiting you,
Would you lament your death?
No matter how bad life's been,
When it comes to your last breath,
Life looks a little better
Than it did a day ago;
You begin to think of things you'd do
if you weren't gonna go.

Would you stampede, if you knew what was to come?
Would you make a break for freedom?
Would you make a break for life?
Show a man his final day; and he'll think twice.

We're men driving cattle;
But we're also driven men.
Knowing where we're going;
Knowing where we're been;
But the purpose of it all?
Well, that's the real question.

In case you're wondering, Yeah! I've had a shot or two.
You ugly, goddamn animals! You don't matter! (*Spoken*) Sorry! Of course, you do.
If the boys hear me talking over things with you,
They'll sell me to the stockyard. I'd make a steak or two.

Did your life make a difference?
How many of our lives actually do?
Even in death your value's not through.
You're going to nourish us. That's why we nourished you.

All that a cowboy leaves behind
 Is a good story or two.
In that way, when you look at it,
I'm not as valuable as you.
        (*Spoken*) Thing is, I've got choices as to what I'll do.

I'm holstering my pistol. I won't spook the herd.
I'm blathering; but you listened and I heard.
I heard how feeling sorry for yourself
is stupid any time of day or year.

Go to sleep, my little dogies, go to sleep.
The Lord above will guard you through the night.
Go to sleep, my little dogies, go to sleep.
I'm here too. I'll care for you. Everything's alright.
        Go to sleep, my little dogies, go to sleep.
        Go to sleep, my little dogies, go to sleep.

(*Recitative*) No wonder we need a trail some fifty plus miles wide
        to get from there to here.
One long-winded cowboy puts out way more bullshit
        than a dozen long-horned steer.

ZOMEGA'S SALOON (Commentary)

Robert E. McGill

My eldest son, Connor Robert, is an accomplished novelist and screenwriter, as well as a scientist. As wide a mind as those accomplishments might suggest, he is not a big fan of poetry and an even less interested patron of Country Western. Consequently, I tried my feeble hand – for I am not a fan of screen-writing – at a "movie" prologue to the song. My hopes were, it might ease his way into the poem. Hope it works for you as well.

FILM PROLOGUE

(Establishing shot from three stories height; and at a distance.)

We see, head on, the length of a small town's main street. It is the old West, early 1800's. The town appears to be deserted; but it is not uninhabited. We can imagine spying eyes behind draped windows. The twilight is fading rapidly; but one establishment, ZOMEGA'S SALOON, is candle - lit from within.

Pacing slowly down the street towards us, are a horse and rider. As the camera arcs down towards them, it pans beside them and then settles in behind. Both the rider and his horse are filthy, as if they'd ridden through a storm of mud. The rider sits askew in the saddle. He lurches with each step his steed takes. Is he exhausted? Is he ailing? His rifle slips from his grip, falling silently on the muddy street. His horse stops on its own, expecting to be commanded back, so that the gun can be fetched. The rider spurs him on.

Outside ZOMEGA'S SALOON, the rider dismounts clumsily. all but falling, sliding down from off his horse. He wraps the horse's bridle around the hitching post of the tavern and staggers towards the door. He pushes through what look to be a saloon's familiar swinging doors.

Now the camera is inside the saloon. We are watching from the Bartender's view. The saloon is lushly furnished, garish; but the wood is polished walnut and the walls are paneled with red velvet. There is a lengthy bar, well appointed, with a capacious stock of liquors on display. There are a half-dozen tables with tablecloths and comfortable chairs available. However, not a single customer is here.

Along with the bartender, we see the horseman, enter through the doors and then, as they shut, slump for support against the door sill.

And so, begins the action.

+

ZOMEGA'S SALOON

Robert E. McGill

C'mon in, Cowboy! Don't be dawdlin' in the door.
That door don't swing no other way than "IN."
Stop leaning up against it, Cowboy. C'mon in.
You look to be as old and cold as sin.

C'mon in, *Vaqueros*! *Andale! Andale! Vamoose!*
Set yourself up at the bar; feel free.
Looks like you could use a drink or two.
The first one's on the house; second's on me;
      (*Spoken*) if you last that long, the third one's free.

I'll get a table ready for you, Cowboy;
Cuz, later on, you'll probably want to eat.
For now, take a stool; and take a load off of your feet.
Water with your whisky? Or do you take yours neat?

Get your ass in here, Cowboy! No more delay!
You've been searching for this place all of your years.
At last you have arrived here at:
      (*Spoken*) 'ZOMEGA'S SALOON AND CAFÉ'.
It was destined that someday you'd end up here.

WHOA! Hold on, Shootist. Leave your weapon at the door!
Oh, never mind. You won't be using it no more.
You finally faced a quicker draw tonight.
Looks like you've fought your last gun fight.

You're hogging precious space, Cowboy! My 'Ladies of Light Virtue,'
My 'Ceiling Gazers' use that door.
But you look so whipped, you'd probably not enjoy
The favors of a good-ole Saloon whore.

I'd rent you a room, Cowboy; but the price is more
Than all your worldly goods are worth.
When Kingdom's Come, it costs a tidy sum
To spend just one last night on Earth.

Cowboy? If you don't mind me asking you a favor,
That wound you're sporting's bleeding on my table.
Could you sit back and tuck this napkin in your chest?
Try cleaning yourself up as best you're able.

Time to stand up, Cowboy; stand up tall.
Time to move on, son; the writing's on the wall.
Hope you're returning home, from whence you came;
If not, you're for the other place or – who knows? – no place at all.

As you're leaving, will you shut the door behind you?
When you're outside, *por favor?* a favor? Scratch a match
And re-light the lantern - it went out before you came -
Beneath the "ZO" in my saloon's name: **ZO***MEGA 'S SALOON.*
        (*Spoken*) My establishment is proud of its true name.

The gunfighter did as he was bid;
And he wept in realizing where he'd came.
His host said, *"Vamoose. Gratias, Amigo! Via con Dios!*
        (*Spoken*) You must, *por favor*, excuse me now.
I must greet a new guest. *OLA! Mi casa su casa!*

 I'm *Zomega.* What's your handle? It's a shame
 I didn't get your predecessor's name.
Pray for him, son. Pray for the forgiveness
Of all your and his regrets. Pray well.
        (*Spoken*) There are no regrets in Heaven. There's nothing *but* in Hell.

THE OLD COWBOY WALTZ

Robert E. McGill

He was a gentleman,
Older than most the men;
Left family and wife to come West.

But he sat his ride handsomely;
All of the boys agreed
He was as good as the best.

In town the boys gambled,
They drank and they rambled;
But he'd bring the place to a halt.

He'd tip the piano man;
Say, "My friend, if you can,
Won't you please play me a waltz?"

      LA-LA, la-**La** la-**La**   **LA-LA**, la- **La** la-**La**
The old cowboy waltzed, one-two- three,
      LA-LA, la-**La** la-**La**   **LA-LA**, la- **La** la-**La**
Come to my arms; dance with me.
      True lovers never prove false
      When they dance the Old Cowboy Waltz

The dance hall girls at the saloon
Would push back the chairs to make room;
'Round they would go, lost in memory's glow
Of the young girls they'd been long ago
      The music forgave all their faults,
      When they danced the Old Cowboy Waltz.

One day a long horn steer
Tore his leg there to here.
He survived the assault with a grin.

He could still ride just fine;
Yet it was quitting time.
He'd knew he'd not waltz again.

Next time he came to town,
His girls all gathered 'round.
They paired up and they waltzed for him.
      LA-**LA**, la-**La** la-**La**   **LA**-**LA**, la- **La** la-**La**
      The old cowboy waltzed, one-two-three,
      LA-**LA**, la-**La** la-**La**   **LA**-**LA**, la- **La** la-**La**
      Won't you come dance with me?
         True lovers never prove false,
         When they dance the Old Cowboy Waltz.

LA BALLADA EL CANYON DEL MUERTE

Robert E. McGill

COOKIE: The Wrangler rode in 'round midnight; and he cried,
"The rivers flooded, no way the herd can cross!"
Eight pair of frightened eyes, eight very tired guys
Turned in despair to their rugged, old trail boss.

"We're two days late already, boys." He said.
"The owners gonna say we broke our word.
"No pay!' they'll say; but you're welcome
 To what's left in the Cook Wagon.
 Divvy that up amongst yourselves. We keep the herd.'"

"But, listen up, boys. I got one, last way to get us there on time.
There's a shortcut that I know, save us sixty miles I'd say.
Thing is, dare you go that way?
Through a place they call, *"El Canyon del Muerte?"*
"El Canon Del Muerte!" I said. "Canyon of Death! Sounds like fun."
Toothpick Rick just shook his head. Threw his hat down on the ground;
Kicked it around; picked it back up and fled.

"He ain't comin' back." I said.
"He's seen The Elephant. He's on the run."
The boys needed the money. "Boss," they said,
"We're fucked either way. Katie, bar the door! Let's get this done!"

And so, it came to pass, that the Wrangler; two thousand head of cattle,
More or less, seven cowboys, *less* toothpick Rick, headed out. (*WAGON WEELS*)
Trail Boss took me, my cook wagon, Ox and all -   (*COW BELLS / SQUEEKS*)
Headed out – Headed up! and headed into *El Canyon del Muerte.*
That was late summer, year of our Lord: Eighteen, Sixty-Two, as I recall.
 Search Party showed up in the fall.

A young V*aquero* said, "I'm riding in.
El Canyon del Muerte! Boo! It's just a name.
It wasn't but a half mile into the cavern
Where he discovered why the searchers came.

There stood the lost herd, frozen in mid stride.
The cowboys on their horses, alongside. Nothing stirred.
You may not believe in Heaven;
But you dasn't dare not - not believe in Hell.
Satan's own incarnate evil had preyed upon this herd. Preyed well.

They stood there like some blasphemous, obscene machine,
Stripped of its cover so that the cogs and gears are seen.
Cowboys, horses, steers: all skeletons! Pristine.
Each and every bone had been picked clean.

The boy's horse shied; kicked a pebble stone.   *(ECHOS OF STONE'S FALL)*
It rambled down the canyon's side.
Its echoes had a life all of their own.
It tumbled until it came to rest against
The lead steer's long silent, bony hoof.

                                        (LIGHNING AND THUNDER)
Then suddenly across the canyon roof
Lightning flashed and thunder crashed!
Heat-lighting inside, in broad daylight!
Something inside this cavern was not right.

The boy's eyes closed in fear; but not his ears. *(HOOVES, SQUEAK OF WAGON WHEELS)*
He heard the shuffling of eight thousand hooves.
When he looked he saw Hell-on-Earth appear.
Madre de Dios! The herd began to move.

     (CRASH AND COLLAPSE OF THE SKELETON HERD)

Just as it did, the whole ghastly, ghostly entourage collapsed
Like the shattering of exquisite, crystal glass,
The shards of which rose up to form a crest
Upon a wave of horror, a wave of animal and human trash
That on an ocean beach – of *El Canyon del Muerte's* floor -
Was poised to crash.   *(Some eerie voices).*

The boy heard ancient voices in the air.
He solved a mystery unsolved until today. *(CHANTING VOICES)*
He screamed. He watched his flesh stripped from his bones,
Eaten alive by *El Canyon del Muerte.*   *(Sudden dead silence)*

Outside, death dust billowed from the canyon.
The search party waited for a time. No one appeared.
"Fire in the hole!" cried the Blast Master.   *(Explosion)*
With a roar the canyon's entrance disappeared. *(Sound tapers off slowly. Silence)*

   "Just whom might I be?
   I'm the 'Cook Wagon Engineer;"
   But most folk call me, 'Cookie. Feel free."
   As to the late mysteries,
   I saw one hell of a hullabaloo. Hell, I saw two.
   I hid out in the wagon
   'til the first horror was through   *(Becoming clear Cookie is quite insane.)*
   The devil rode through on a horse that he called, "Blue."

He turned everything to glass.
I hid in the cook wagon, or I'd have a shiny, crystal ass.

I Lived on what was left in the cook wagon.
As I recall, I ate a lot of stew.
Then came the rescue party;
Another round of horror I lived through.

I rode out on the Vaquero's horse.
Had to go back around, took a day or two.
El Canyon del Muerto.
On hell of a short cut to cut short your life.
What a pity. What a loss.
If That god-damn river hadn't flooded,
We might have got across.

COOKIE: That's all I have to say, your Honor.   *(He rises to leave)*
(*As an afterthought*) No one ever goes there. No one dares.
They say, "You can't pay me enough to set foot there."   *(vocal "wind")*
But I do. Cuz, if you're ever near those Godforsaken environs;
And the wind is right,   *(Start musical and vocal "screaming")"*
You can hear the boys and cattle
Screaming through the night and well into the day.

> (***CLIMAX!*** *Hold one long note.* Cookie *looks at his hands, extending them away from himself, in terror, as he did when describing the young* Vaquero's *death, as if his flesh was being stripped away. Chord ends suddenly.* Cookie *wiggles his fingers and says,* "DON'T WORRY! I'M OK!")

CHAPTER 2:

DEMON RUM: Sometimes Funny; Always Tragic

A LITTLE SHOT OF WHISKY

Robert E. McGill

[This is a song as well as a theatrical performance piece. It is unique and demanding.
Consequently, I am suggesting basic stage directions for an approach to presenting the work.
We are in brightly lit, concert form. The accompaniment is electronic, and the tempo is lively.]

A little shot of whisky makes a big shot fool of me.
I'm ten feet tall and frisky, and as handsome as can be.
The only trouble is that everyone but me,
Sees that if I down some Royal Crown it makes a clown of me.

I hit on all the women. They're too shy to hit on me.
In their ears I whisper some mild obscenities.
Some slap, some cry, all eventually flee.
They're all intimidated by my masculinity.

I pass the time by singing some fine karaoke;
I am cool at hustling pool. I take down a rookie.
I have a little more to drink to charge my battery;
And I brag to the barkeep of my unique supremacy

[Here there is a slow and dramatic change. The bright, concert lights segue to a gentle blue. We are entering the inner life of the performer. The music changes to acoustic guitar, flute, cello, piano. The performer can sing to a poignant melody or recite.]

I am a sad and lonely clown.
My heart shattered with remorse.
Jesus, help me. I wish I could change course;
But I just can't put that goddamn bottle down

[And now we resume bright light concert form and music. From here on, the indented passages are all in the 'private' mode.]

Now those women's men-folk come back in with a crash.
Their dares, insults and taunts are particularly brash.
I say, "Boys! I'm innocent! They offered sex for cash.
Let's talk about your women if you want to talk real trash."

I've been offered my salvation, but I've always turned it down;
But misery is optional. I don't have to be a clown.
The memory of my life should be erased from history;
Yet; I hear the voice of Jesus. He's not given up on me.

Well those good old boys - all "Bubbas,"- kick the dying daylights out of me.
They leave me in the parking lot, close to eternity.
When I wake up next morning, I find my car door's key.
I carry a survival kit, a half-pint of whisky.

Despair and fear and desperate prayer breed true humility.
I didn't drink that morning. I asked Christ to rescue me.
First, I have to shed my clown face; and I must stop fooling me.
There's still time for atonement. May that be my destiny.

I fear the terrors of cold turkey
The body shakes and spasms.
No sleep, no nourishment;
Visitations from phantasms.

The mind recites an endless list
Of all you've lost, of all you've missed.
There's self-contempt and grieving for the host
Of crimes committed on those who loved you most.

*[A new mode here: a combination of the internal mode with a resurrection
and hope of the bright lights and triumphant conclusion.]*

But the world of hurt I've created breeds some small humility.
I will make apologies and perform atonement
Sweet Jesus, hold my hand and, Lord look over me.
And all of you, I pray for you. Won't you please pray for me?

Help me put the goddamn bottle down.

DEMON WHISKEY'S SPELL

Robert E. McGill

I don't know what I'm gonna do tomorrow.
Be a good day to wallow in my sorrow.
But today is Saturday, all day.
School is out. I want to play.
Companionship I'll either beg or borrow.

Who knows? I may not live to see Sunday.
     (*Spoken*) Now there's a reason to start drinking right away.
I could be some mad killer's prey,
Or struck by a meteor shower.
I can't afford to waste another hour.
It's Saturday, man. Let's get underway.

I'll start the morning with a Bloody Mary.
Maybe two - or three - enough to carry
Me until high noon or near;
Then I'll have a couple beers.
For now, look in the mirror. It's Bloody Mary!

     We're all under Demon Whiskey's spell.
     You may hide your feelings from the public very well;
     But we're all inside some private kind of Hell.
     We're all under Demon Whisky's spell.

     Don't you understand? You've shaken Satan's hand.
     You play his games. You drink his favorite brand.
     We all smell that Goddamn brimstone smell.
     We're all under Demon Whiskey's spell.
          (*Spoken*) And, Boy, he's waiting for us both deep down in Hell.

I'll visit The Casino this afternoon.
I don't want to get wasted any too soon.
You're sure to take a loss
If you gamble on the sauce.
I'll drink whisky, but I'll drink it from a spoon.

An *aperitif* to stir my appetite;
A postprandial *liqueur* to greet the night.
I had some milk with dinner,
So, I'm free to be a sinner.
We played all day; I'm good to go all night.

There's a Saloon called ZOMEGA'S with a Western theme.
I'll pick up a cowgirl and propose my scheme.
An evening of drinking and delight!
We three will dance away the night.
My new best girl, myself and ole Jim Beam

We're all under Demon Whiskey's spell.
      You hide your feelings from the public well;
      But we're all inside some private kind of Hell.
      We're all under Demon Whisky's spell.

      Don't you understand? You've shaken Satan's hand.
      You play his games. You drink his favorite brand.
      We all smell that Goddamn brimstone smell.
      We're all under Demon Whiskey's spell.
          (*Spoken*) And, Boy, he's waiting for us both deep down in Hell.

I cannot, do not recommend my life style.
I can't defend it. Not by a country mile.
But try walking in my shoes;
Inside a quarter mile; you'll smile.
      (*Spoken*) You'll recognize you've been me all the while.

      We're all under Demon Whiskey's spell.
      You hide your feelings from the public well;
      But we're all inside some private kind of Hell.
      We're all under Demon Whisky's spell.

      Don't you understand? You've shaken Satan's hand.
      You play his games. You drink his favorite brand.
      We all smell that goddamn brimstone smell.
      We're all under Demon Whiskey's spell.
          (*Spoken*) And, Boy, he's waiting for us both deep down in Hell.

TURN OUT THE LIGHTS AND RAISE THE ROOF

Robert E. McGill

I'm eighty-seven dollars overdrawn
Down at the bank.
There's nothin' in the fridge to eat;
There's no gas in the tank.

They'll be shutting off my water:
Makes it hard to keep cleanly.
They'll be turning off my power.
Fetch the candles.
       (*Spoken*) Farewell, DIRECT TV.

I'd get a job, but what I'd make
- Even if I worked two -
Wouldn't take a bite out of
The debt I have to chew.

       My taste is for *Courvoisier*.
       Hell, anything that's 80 proof.
       Give me whiskey; I'm a carpenter.
       Trust me, I'll raise the roof.

I'd like to blame my last boss,
The one who fired me.
I'd like to blame the broken heart
You smashed when you left me.

I'd like to blame a lot of things
But most of them are mine.
The way I've led my life
Should convict me of a crime.

Don't think I can't stop drinking.
I've done it many times; Alas! in vain.
The moment I'm stone cold sober dry,
I toast my new found freedom with CHAMPAIGNE.
       (*Spoken*) And here we go again!

My taste is for *Courvoisier*;
Hell, anything that's 80 proof.
Give me whiskey; I'm a carpenter.
Stand aside, I'll raise the roof.

And though I'm walking with my shoulders closer to the ground,
I may be temporarily out; but I'm not permanently down.
Give your last dollar to someone needier than you
Pray for me my brother and my sister; and I will pray for you.
Love each other – even those you don't know -
And trust we're gonna make it through.
Christ was a carpenter too.

GIVE ME A BREAK

Robert E. McGill

I demand I take my break 'round Ten or so.
A cold beer; and I'm right back, early: Good to go.
Come noon, for lunch, I'll have a brew or two.
Those and a couple tokes will get me through.

Let's all cheer the time-honored coffee break!
'Course coffee's not the only thing I take.
I really think, at work, I'm of more use
When I'm just a little high on weed and booze.

It's hard to find a place to smoke these days.
Like we were kids, we meet in alleyways.
Well, "What goes around, comes around!" They say.
I'm eighth grade; wrapped in marijuana haze.

Until Three o'clock, nothing can hurt me.
Well, tell the truth, I do break 'round Two-Thirty.
I knock back a shot or two then. Keeps me alive
Until that 'Break-Free" whistle blows at five.

I'm not stupid. I know I'm gonna lose this job.
They'll say, "Pee in this bottle." To my sorrow
No gold watch for me. No gold watch fob.
They'll say, "You're fired." Don't come back tomorrow.

Before that happens, I may have an accident.
I might get injured working my work station.
Cut off my little finger's tip and need an operation.
Then retire on Workman's Compensation.

> (*Spoken*) As someone - *Johnny Paycheck* - famously said:
> "You can take this break and shove it!
> I'm on permanent vacation!"

NOTE: What follows are my comments on the song that I'm sharing with my colleague//composer//performer, Kasey Yeargain. He often teased me about "preaching."

"Kasey, I think you'll like this ending. I don't think we really want to follow him on a downward spiral. Why not let the rascal get by? 😊 See, I can leave Preacher Bob out of the picture! 😊 These are your words; and I'd remember them, by way of introducing the song: **"I think this is an ode to the modern-day rebel trapped in a cubicle."** That's a real tribute and insight. "Cubicle" might not be just the right word. I do know from spending time at AA meetings and in recovery that the mind and soul killing boredom, repetition and apparent meaninglessness of work can destroy a soul. Cubicle implies at the very least a white-collar job. This guy's blue collar. Something like, "anyone trapped in a . . . . ? on an Assembly Line?

I WAKE UP TO A HARSH REALITY

Robert E. McGill

PROEM:
> *REALITY IS I'VE NO GAS LEFT IN MY HEART – MORE OR LESS MY TRUCK..*
> *REALITY'S I'VE LOST MY GAL; REALITY'S A DISMAL "F . . . , or (REALITY CAN SUCK)*
> *YOU REACH ME A LONG NECK, IF YOU'D BE SO KIND?*
> *I'LL REACH FOR THE LONG NECK OF MY GUITAR;*
> *I'LL SING SOME SONGS TO GET HER OFF MY MIND.*

Reality's I wake up to a harsh reality.
 I wake up to the scratching of a mouse.
He flees from me. Reality's I wake up
To a messed-up room, a messed-up house.
Reality's I wake up to a messed-up me.
. . . . . I reach for my guitar.

I wake up without my morning star.
She fled from me - was it only - one week ago?
        (*Spoken*) Since then, I've been going-south real fast; real far.
I wake up to a harsh reality;
For me, reality's a bridge too far.
. . . . . I reach for my guitar.

        I pick up my guitar; I strum a chord;
                I find my peace! Sweet Jesus, thank you Lord!
                    In my music's fantasy,
                        I deny reality;
                            I'm captain of my destiny;
                                Life's as it ought to be;
                                    And nothing's wrong with me.

        If there's one place I belong, it's inside of my own song.
        Best thing of all is: Catherine's still here with me.

Reality's I'm drinking by dawn's light;
Yeah! And smoking grass by afternoon.
Reality's if she doesn't come back soon,
I'll be howling like a mad coyote at the moon.
Lost track of when I lost my appetite.
. . . . . I pick up my guitar. (*Spoken*) I've got a song to write.

Maybe if I sing about what she's doing now;
Where she might be; exactly who she's with.

I'll forget about her teaching me to kiss:
How her parted lips could thrust and cuddle
Like a witchy woman's hips.
. . . . . I pick up my guitar.
I pick up my guitar; I strum a chord;
      I find my peace! Sweet Jesus, thank you Lord!
        In my music's fantasy,
          I deny reality;
            I'm captain of my destiny;
              Life's as it ought to be;
                And nothing's wrong with me.

    If there's one place I belong, it's inside of my own song.
    Best thing of all is: Catherine's still here with me.

She left her key behind; but I don't lock the door.
I lay awake and listen for its squeak.
The mouse squeaks. All that's louder is the sound of
My scratching for the memories of her love.
Will I hear her footsteps on our bedroom floor?
. . . . . I reach for my guitar.

Who am I kidding? She's not coming home.
"Never. Never. Never. Never. Never."[i]
Wake up! to your harsh reality: "She'll come no more."[ii]
Wake up! There'll be no creak of our front door.
Reality's - without her - what am I living for?
. . . . . I drop the mic. I put down my guitar

        END

    *(IF Proem is used, then **THIS** should be the final verse.)*

Wake up! Who you fooling? "She'll come no more."[iii]
"Never. Never. Never. Never. Never."[iv]
Will there be a creak at our front door.
What am I living for? She's gone forever.
I'm just this side of suicide. Other side's not far.
      (Spoken) Where's that Dude, bought me a beer? Still here?
. . . . . I drop the mic. Take care of my guitar.

---

[i] Shakespeare, William. KING LEAR, V.iii.

[ii] Shakespeare, William. KING LEAR, V.iii.

[iii] Shakespeare, William. KING LEAR, V.iii.

[iv] Shakespeare, William. KING LEAR, V.iii.

WHEN YOU'RE DRINKING LONELY
Robert E. McGill

Knock back that shot of whiskey;
And chase it with a beer.
My songs smooth the booze. (*Spoken*) So choose your poison.
What would you like to hear?

Rim that tequila glass with salt,
Wet your hand and pour some there;
Lick salt, suck lime. *Salud!* (*Performer can make a "Brrrr" straight whiskey shiver*)
Straight tequila earns you a fanfare.

Skoal! Bottom's up! Music deserves a toast.
I love to hear those glasses clink.
It's magic. I keep sounding better,
Every time you have a drink.

When you're drinking lonely, your best companion is a song.
It won't quarrel, get up and leave you; or tell you that you're wrong.
No matter how drunk you want to get, it just wants to get along.
Good thing too. The evening's young. Lots of time. Things can go wrong.
(*Spoken*) When you're drinking lonely, your best companion is a song.

A song will listen, laugh and cry with you; So whatcha wanna hear?
If I don't know it, hum it; I can pick it up by ear.
A melody can lullaby a broken heart or make it strong.
Booze and music tend to harmonize love songs. Just sing along.
But I know the only song you solo drinkers want to hear
Goes, *"I'll always love you gal. Why can't you be here?"*

So, sip your wine or mixed drink;
And may my melodies
Accompany your every mood
From joy to sympathy.

When you're drinking lonely,
Music mellows out what's wrong.
Maybe tonight, you'll meet Mz. or Mr. Right.
'Til then, your best companion is a song.

When you're drinking lonely, your best companion is a song.
It won't quarrel, get up and leave you; or tell you that you're wrong.
No matter how drunk you want to get, it just wants to get along.
(*Spoken*) When you're drinking lonely, your best companion is a song.
But I know the only song you solo drinkers want to hear
Goes, *"I'll always love you gal. Why can't you be here?"*
When you're drinking lonely, your best companion is a song.

DEATH ROW: WHISKEY PRISON
(Long line / short line versions)
Robert E. McGill

Warden, they're getting set to murder me.
They say that today's my last and dying day.
You know that, truth be told, I'm innocent;
I know you know that's what I always say.

Warden, they're going to kill me.
They say today's my dying day.
You know I didn't do it.
I know you know that's what I say.

There's time yet for the governor to pardon;
I'm not hopin' for. It don't look that way.
I'm feelin' all kinds of awful twitchy.
Warden I need some whiskey right away.

The Guv'nor might still pardon me;
But it don't look that way.
I'm all kinds of twitchy, Boss.
How 'bout some whisky right away?

CHORUS

When I was still a young man,
I never thought I'd see
The heartache and the terror
Caused by whisky; caused by me.

No one plans to be a drunkard.
No one hopes to rob a bank.
No one wants to kill a man.
I've got whiskey to blame.
(*Spoken*) I've got myself to thank.

I ain't hungry for no gourmet final meal.
I don't mind goin' hungry to my grave.
A couple double shots of Crown Royal Seagram's
The final earthly pleasure that I crave.

I don't want no last meal.
I'll go hungry to my grave.
A double shot of Seagram's Seven's
The last earthly joy I crave.

Warden, please spare me that smarmy Chaplain?
My soul's beyond his abilities to save.
I've had my fill of, "Come to Jesus!" lectures.
Give me my whisky, Warden, right away.

And I don't want no Chaplain
My soul tryin' to save.
I don't need lectures, Warden.
I need whiskey right away.

So long, my death row cell mates all.
I'm free at last, Good God! At last I'm free.
If you ever manage to get out of here
Won't you drink a toast or two in memory?
Drink Uisce Beatha (**eesch** *ge* **ba***ha*)
That's Gaelic for 'whiskey.'

So long, my death row buddies.
I'm gonna finally be free.
If someday, they turn you loose
You drink a whiskey toast to me.

CHORUS

When I was still a young man,
I never thought I'd see
The heartache and the terror
Caused by whisky; caused by me.
No one plans to be a drunkard.
No one hopes to rob a bank.
No one wants to kill a man.
I've got whiskey to blame.
(*Spoken*) I've got myself to thank.

I ain't got no family here to visit me,	I don't got no family,
'Cept those who couldn't wait to come and see	'Cept those that came to see
My soul's departure to eternity.	My soul depart for Hell.
Let's hope the Devil's whisky welcomes me.	I hear the Devil serves whiskey.
I've spent my life on Death Row: Whisky Prison.	I spent my life in Whisky Prison
Oh, I tried many times many a break.	I tried many a break
But you can't leave the thing you love	I couldn't leave my drink behind.
or (But I couldn't leave that bottle far behind)	
Whisky, Warden! Mellow out my last escape.	Whiskey, Warden! Help me escape

THE END
(You might consider this <u>voice over/sound effects</u> ending.)

Slam of prison cell closing.
Scraping of ankle chains dragging.
      CHAPLAIN: "My son, the Lord Jesus . . ."
      PRISONER: "No thanks, Father."
          OTHER PRISONER VOICES: "Dead man walking! Dead man walking!"

EXTRA VERSE: (*If needed or wanted*)

I've been in whisky prison most 'my life.
Married to my bottle like you're married to your wife;
'Cept there's no divorce permitted me,
No peaceful separation. DEATH ROW: WHISKY PRISON
    (*Spoken*) My lifelong incarceration. Hell of a final destination.

CHAPTER 3:

SPECIALTY SONGS: *Tricks & Gimmicks*

DON'T THROW ME UNDERNEATH THE BUS!
Robert E. McGill

(*Spoken*) **PLEASE**! **Darling,**

(*Song begins*)

PLEASE! Don't throw me underneath the bus! *Bah-Dump! / Bah-Dump!*
I know what that means and how it feels.
I cheated on you! One colossal blunder;
And I set your universe a-reel.

I think you want me under
Some really rig-rous wheels.
You want them to tear me asunder.
But if there's a chance we could once again be us,
      Please, Darling Girl, don't throw me underneath the bus.

We've all of us been thrown underneath the bus. Bombs away! *Bah-Dump! / Bah-Dump! /*
I'll bet you've all thrown one or two. *Bah-Dump! Bah-Dump! / Bah-Dump! Bah-Dump!*
Not nice to see: *(very quickly) Bah-Dump! Bah-Dump! / Bah-Dump! Bah-Dump! / Bah-Dump! Bah-Dump!*
      (*Spoken*) I've thrown three.

CHORUS
Without you, throw me most anywhere! Who cares?
'Over the rainbow,' 'aside,' 'out,' or 'for a loop' or 'for a loss.'
Throw me off a bronco bull or bucking hoss.
I'll punch my final ticket. I'll pay my final fare.
If there's no future for the two of us,
I'm glad to perish underneath a bus

"Thrown underneath the bus." an old cliché: a "throw away!"
Here's the question that puzzles me.
It's right up there with "To be or not to be?"
It's "How would you actually do it, if you did it actually?

How would you do it anyway?
Have you thought of that?
You're 94 pounds dripping wet;
I'm more than twice times that.

Would you run up from behind me
At full speed and heave;
Or are you in the driver's seat,
Preparing me to leave?

Would you throw me out the door;
Then curve me back, beneath the floor?
That's quite a trick to have tucked up your sleeve.
If you throw "stuff" like that without fatigue,
    (*Spoken*) You should be pitching in the major leagues.

CHORUS
    Without you, throw me most anywhere! Who cares?
    'Over the rainbow,' 'aside,' 'out,' or 'for a loop' or 'for a loss.'
    Throw me off a bronco bull or bucking hoss.
    I'll punch my final ticket. I'll pay my final fare.
    If there's no future for the two of us,
    I'm glad to perish underneath a bus

Once I'm underneath, do you plan on running *OVER* me? *(Bah-dump! Bah-dump!)*
Mangle legs, crack ribs; mash limbs, divide me at the waist?
You'll grind me, 'til there's nothing left but paste.
My skull will squirt out brains; but what a waste!

I love you! Won't you grant me one more try?
Let your wrath benignly pass me by?   (Next line sung to melody of ***1ˢᵗ NOEL***)
Like angels did sing to this certain poor shepherd
(*Spoken*) Don't throw me underneath the bus. *(resume carol melody)* I don't want to
die.

If you're gonna do it, do it right.
Best back up over me to seal the deal; *Bah-Dump! Bah-Dump! /*
Or do a "Wheelie" on me. Peal and squeal. *Bah-Dump! Bah-Dump! /*
    (*All Band*) *'Gunning' engine roars. Body parts being minced and spit out. Ten beats.*
    *Louder, LOUDER, **LOUDER**! – Full stop!* <u>*Silence)*</u>
      (*Spoken*) Now that was real!

Rueful silence. The dreadful deed's complete.
A crime of passion, done in passion's heat.
Will you regret; will you deplore
Your evil act or will it be ignored?
    (*Spoken*) Will you leave flowers in my empty seat?

CHORUS
    Without you, throw me most anywhere! Who cares?
    'Over the rainbow,' 'aside,' 'out,' or 'for a loop' or 'for a loss.'
    Throw me off a bronco bull or bucking hoss.
    I'll punch my final ticket. I'll pay my final fare.
    If there's no future for the two of us,
    I'm glad to perish underneath a bus

If there's no hope that we can once again be us,
I'll die at my own hand I'll throw *myself* underneath the bus.
If there's no chance, you'll take me back I'll gladly jump.
I don't want to end my life as a speed bump.
NO, I DON'T WANT TO END MY LIFE AS A SPEED BUMP!

Darling, Honey Girl, I am so sorry.
Love me again? Don't throw me underneath the bus.

HOLE-IN-ONE
Robert E. McGill

The eighteenth tee. The Masters.
Thousands hold their breath as one.
They're all hoping to be witness
To a fabled hole-in-one.

> (*Spoken*) So I stood, in breathless silence,
> In that crowd, when I saw her.

I knew my quest for Romance
Could, at last, be done.
My heart would be complete and whole
If *her* heart could be won.

But she drove away and left me;
Told me cruel lies from the start.
She liked riding in Mercedes.

> (*Spoken: in a Golf Announcer's whispered voice*:
> "Official vehicle of the LPGA!")

I was driving a golf cart.

I made some good approaches;
But none were up to par.
I never holed that final putt.
I never got that far.

Her trophies were men's broken hearts.
Her lovers were undone.
When offers of true love arose,
She'd poke a hole in one.

Her reckless ways were not unnoticed.
She was a golf ball on God's tee.
He swung his terrible swift driver;
Sliced her to eternity.

There, she faced the ultimate scorekeeper.
He counted her life's sum.
"There are 18 horrid cells in Hell" he said
"You've earned a hole in one."

I LIKE TO RIDE THE BUS
Robert E. McGill
Dedicated to Rick Spahr

Since we human beings been around,
We've loved to find a way to ride on things.
Adam and Eve rode bareback (*Spoken:* Quite a sight!)
On Unicorns with wings. Until the Mighty
Good Lord roared, "Dismount! I've found you out!
 "Come out of hiding; No more riding. Take a hike!"
Since then we've ridden horses. What's not to like?

CHORUS

I like to ride the bus. I like the bus.
It makes me feel like I am one of us;
And some days when I'm lonely,
Or frightened, lacking company;
The bus ride makes *us* one with me.

Now once we've graduated snow boards, pogo sticks and skis,
Trains, boats, airplanes and all things wearing wheels,
We are finally ready to select automobiles.
Some folk like limousines, Audis, Lexus, Beemers;
Some prefer a racing car, a Porsche, a Lamborghini.
Others less adventurous, drive Eco-friendly, fix-me-ups
Or a "Bubba" pickup truck. Me? I like the bus.

CHORUS

I like the bus. I like the bus.
It makes me feel like I am one of us
And some days when I'm lonely,
Or frightened, lacking company;
The bus ride makes *us* one with me.

The scenery, outside and in, is always picturesque.
There're people playing music, rapping; sometimes you hear a cuss;
But the price is neat, FREE can't be beat. I like to ride the bus.
We drive to work, pick up, deliver and to let our neighbors see
Just how less happy and far worser off they are than we.
BUT We're all riding the same highway to that same terminal station.
I ridden every vehicle, travelled every way you can to that destination.

It's riding, listening, watching on the bus where
I've come to understand we're all the same.
Some hardcore sinners, a few saints; but most are plain and fine.
I see the best, worst, in-between; and say, "All this is mine,"
Amidst the camaraderie of these striving folk I love.
Is there any better way to pass life's time?
How we hitch-hike, speed or crawl along life's journey's up to us.
Of all the ways to go, I'll ride the bus.

CHORUS

> I like to ride the bus. I like the bus.
> It makes me feel like I am one of us
> And some days when I'm lonely,
> Or frightened, lacking company;
> The bus ride makes *us* one with me.

We the people can be rowdy; but things always calm down.
'long as we're in the same bus/boat, you rarely see a frown.
I look around; the light and sound of comedy and tragedy.
It's totally unscripted, realer than reality tv.
Some are clutching grocery bags, some clutch one another.
Some are clutching lonely secrets, all alone; yet one of us.
All this is mine: aromas from the smorgasbord of our humanity.
I like to ride the bus. It makes *us* one with me.

CHORUS

> I like to ride the bus. I like the bus.
> It makes me feel like I am one of us
> And some days when I'm lonely,
> Or frightened, lacking company;
> The bus ride makes *us* one with me.

I NEVER THOUGHT I'D FALL IN LOVE WITH YOU
Robert E. McGill

Holy Moses, On a Crutch! Girl! Girl, How *Do* You Do?
I never thought I'd fall in love with you.
There's nothing special I find in your features;
Yet true love's found and bound us:
      (*Spoken*) Two very different creatures.

We don't have much in common. We don't talk.
On any normal day I'd say, "Go, take a walk!"
You're the last one on the planet I'd turn to;
But now I find myself enthralled by you.

Looks like you like me enough to stay:
But you'll sit down and hush up when I say.

     A) In everything my will must be obeyed.
        If you're down with that, then we're OK.
(*or*)
     B) I'm the guy decides our 'YES' or 'NO.'
     If You're down with that, we're good to go.

I never viewed your face or figure with desire;
But then your eyes flamed, igniting passion's fire.
Your wet kisses tantalized my tongue.
You whimpered; my resistance came undone.

I can't imagine what you see in me.
I'm not overly good looking or friendly.
But you weren't shy; you shook your butt at me.
Next moment we were petting heavily.

Your hairs a mess. You need a bath. You stink;
But I'm not all that house-broke, come to think.
The S.P.C.A. owes me one big, "Hooray!"
Let's go home, my brand-new doggie.
     Here, girl. (*PAUSE; then gently*) STAY!

(Reprise) I never thought I'd fall in love with you.
     Finis

ENCORE?

You wanna listen to it, one more time?
It's a silly-willy song;
But more fun, the more you know what's going on.
Here we go. I'll play real slow.
Raise your hands when first you know
What you should have known first time ago.

POUR VOUS, SENOR RAGUENEAU
Robert E. McGill
based on Lope de Vega's FUENTE OVEJUNA. Mengo

A POET'S A STREET VENDOR,
SELLING FRESH MADE MELODIES.
HE ROUGHLY SHAPES HIS DOUGH;
GIVES HIS PASTERIES A THROW
INTO HIS KETTLE'S BOILING
OIL OF CREATIVITY.

MOST OF HIS SHODDY TRIES
AREN'T FIT FOR HUMAN TASTE
OR SMELL, NOT TO MENTION HUMAN EYES.
SOME ARE *OVER* COOKED; SOME OTHERS . . . *UNDER*;
BUT WHEN ONE TURNS OUT WELL SHAPED,
SUBSTANIAL, TASTY, WORTHY TO BE TAKEN HOME,
THE BAKER'S QUEST IS ENDED. *VOILA! OLE!*
HE'S FINALLY MADE A POEM.

BUT WE FEIGN HUMILITY. WE BAKER POETS
DON'T OWN UP TO OUR OWN POETRY.
THOUGH WE KNOW IT, WE CLAIM NOT TO SHOW IT.
WE PROFESS TO BE ONLY A MERE STREET VENDOR,
A *QUONDAM JONGLEUR*? PERHAPS; BUT NOT A POET,
NO MORE THAN THE LOCAL FRIAR IS THE POPE!
BUT BOTH BAKER AND THE REVEREND MONK
MUST NOT BE DENIED THEIR HOPE.
BOTH OFFER NOURISHMENT TO KEEP US WHOLE:
THE CHEF, A VENDOR FOR THE BODY;
 THE FRIAR, A MENDER FOR THE SOUL.

THEY REPRESENT THEIR MAKER'S LOVE OF MAKING;
THE JOYS OF BAKING AND CREATION TOO.
FRIAR, I CONFESS! A *GOOD* POEM'S A *GREAT* TEMPTATION.
I'D SELL MY SOUL – WELL, MAYBE A DONUT OR TWO –
TO MAKE ANOTHER. GREAT GOD! BUT IT'S FUN.
FORGIVE ME, MY SINS, FATHER.
CROSS MY PALM WITH SILVER!
OR A *PESO* OR A *SOU* OR TWO;
I'LL MAKE YOU ANOTHER ONE.

YOU KNOW YOU'D LOVE ANOTHER ONE.

CHAPTER 4:

STORY SONGS

FIRST TIME IT SNOWS
Robert E. McGill
For Clancy and Tony Dark

What do I want? I want to go back home.
There's a ramshackle cottage that I own.
I'll get a dog. We won't be that alone.
We'll be fine, we two, out there on our own.

I'd like to fly-fish; let what I catch go.
I want to ask the forest what it knows.
I need to follow where the river goes.
I've got to be back home first time it snows.

I'd like to sleep out underneath the stars,
Far from city lights and city bars.
I want to watch the meteorites fall.
I need to be just one but part of all.

    Comes a time, you just gotta let it go:
    All the "should-haves, could-haves," that you'll never know.
    Wisdom arrives too late. Time's river flows.
    You've got to be back home before it snows.

I'll bet that I can still lay a trout line.
I can harvest a deer. That would be fine.
I can live off the land. Good thing to know.
I will be back home before it snows.

I'd like to cut a dozen cords of wood.
I want to cut some cords here 'fore I go.
I need to find a thousand bucks or so.
But I will be back home first time it snows.

    Comes a time, you just gotta let it go:
    All the "should haves, could haves," that you'll never know.
    Wisdom comes too late. Time's river flows.
    You've got to be back home first time it snows.

I'm needing to be home first time it snows
I'm needing to remember long-agos.
Love was year-round until she had to go.
I'll find her there again first time it snows.

NOTE: *to "Clancy," Kathleen McGill, my Sister, and "Tony Dark," my Ophelia*

This has evolved rather nicely, I believe. That is no small part due to both of your sensitive criticisms. I hope you will see your efforts reflected in a not quite - but almost - finished work.

Whenever I was inquiring of actors, in class or rehearsal, what it was their characters were seeking, I would often be told some version of, "He's just . . . / She's only . . ."

I would challenge them on that. "Just" and "only" ain't enough to hold center stage.

I'd ask of the class or cast, "How many of you would _like_ to write a novel?" All hands up. "How many of you _want_ to write a novel?" One third of all hands up. "How many of you _must / have to_ write a novel?" Two or three hands.

I would say to them, "Then you will."

Love, God, Blood, Sex and Death: "the two-hour traffic of our stage." Desire must be as fierce, beyond all previous experience, to perform the extraordinary human behavior portrayed in the theatre; and, when we recall first snowfalls, sometimes in life.

MAMA'S HERE

Robert E. McGill

Everything was too bright; shiny.
Snow was swirling all around.
The sky was shiny too: bright blue.
The flakes refused to reach the ground.

They must be frozen angel tears.
They must have come from heaven.
It was my Mother's funeral.
It was cold, and I was seven.

"How long will I be so sad, Dad?
How long will I be missing her?"
"Until the day you die, my son;
But not the kind of sad that hurts."

    (Spoken) "Dad said,) "In time your grief will turn to laughter.
    Mom will only be away a little while.
    Soon she'll be here with us forever after.
    We'll know she's here, the first time that we smile."

"We'll smile when we remember happy memories.
How Mom would wield that garden hose.
No one who came near could come away
With anything resembling dry clothes.

She loved playing pranks on April Fool's Day.
All day long, her mischief would appear.
Once she set our clock's ahead an hour.
We forgave her; but it took about a year.

    (Spoken) Dad said, "In time your grief will turn to laughter.
    Mom will only be away a little while.
    Soon she'll be here with us forever after.
    We'll know she's here the first time that we smile.

She taught you how to cook and sew and pray;
And when you do, she's there with you to help
You understand the language of the heart.
That's how you'll talk to her though you're apart.

She'll know your problem in advance;
She always knows mine through and through.
I still talk to my Mom every day;
Soon, son, you'll talk to your Mom too.

    The tears of angel's snowflakes
    Fell and rested on the ground.
    I knew that I would never fear.
    Mom's gone away a little while; (*Pause*)
    (*Spoken*) I'm smiling. Mama's here.

NEW GIRL IN TOWN
Robert E. McGill

She rented rooms up at the boarding house,
A classy place of local high renown.
It took a little while before she styled
Her way into the local bar downtown.

In her black dress, high heels and simple pearls,
She was more than just a trifle out of place.
In our smoky, run down, honky-tonk cafe
And bar: famous for its parquet dancing space.

She realized this was not a cocktail lounge.
She picked up quick the local gals' dress code.
No more movie star sheik chic for her.
She blew away the place next time she showed.

She wore a denim mini-skirt and boots.
She couldn't bring herself to do "big hair."
But she filled out her flannel shirt and leather vest;
She wore her ponytail with cowgirl flair.

The local beauties flashed their jealous eyes.
She shone like Cinderella at the ball.
You didn't need to ask a magic mirror
To know she was the fairest of them all.

We guys are shy. Her kind of awesome beauty
Is attractive but intimidates romance.
No one – not even on a dare – would ask her
If she'd like to have a beer or share a dance.

She'd had enough of sitting there alone.
She took her bull by its two horns; that bull was me.
She walked right over to my solo table (*Spoken*) She said,
You're here stag, like me. How's 'bout some company?
  (*Spoken*) And she went on,

"The Lord alone knows – he should: He made us.
And surely, we're not made to be alone.
If I'm way out of line by saying, "Hey!" to you,
 him who's never wept throw the first stone.
        (*Spoken*) Do you suppose I might sit down 'side you?"

Most times my social graces fail with women.
This time I knew exactly what to do.
I rose, pulled out her chair – (*Spoken*) *Mama would have been so proud.* I said,
"I'd be honored if you'd join me. Please have a seat, won't you?"

She sprung for our first round; when that was done
She said, "I'm gonna give you your big chance.
You owe me one. Don't fret, it should be fun.
Teach me to do that Texas Two-Step dance.

I waltzed that lady onto the dance floor.
We danced real close and slow. I'd not let go.
I knew I'd found the only one for me.
We wed a couple kids or so ago.
        (*Spoken*) How she learned *that* Texas Two-Step, I don't know.

I do know when I see a body looking lonely,
Sitting solo in a bar or on a bus,
I take the chance my Lady took on me.
I make that lonely stranger one of us.
        (*Spoken*) And I say,

"The Lord alone knows – he should: He made us.
 And surely, we're not made to be alone.
If I'm way out of line saying, "Hey!" to you,
 Let him who's never wept throw the first stone.
        (*Spoken*) Do you suppose I might sit down'side you?"

SUPER HERO
Robert E. McGill

I was playing Super Hero,
Jumping off my Grandma's porch.
From a tired towel, she'd made a cape;
I'd painted on a torch.

I was hoping to be "FLAME MAN;"
But I couldn't learn to fly.
That's when my Daddy came along -
Pretending - that he hadn't seen me cry.
He had a word to say.

> "You're not a super hero, son;
> No more so than I;
> (*Spoken*) And that raggedy-ass towel won't make you one.
> You've got no super powers to disguise.
>
> You won't always be the best. No lie.
> But, son, you do the best you can.
> That's how you'll learn to fly;
> And how to be a super, super Man."

I thought my Daddy was a fool.
By God! I *would* be best!
I learned quick I wasn't perfect;
But I pretended to the rest

That it didn't really matter.
When it came time to do my best,
I'd set no standards for myself.
I sorely flunked life's test.

I dropped out of College;
Lost Dad's farm back to the bank;
I was discharged dishonorably;
Watched my first marriage tank.

Dad knew my soul was crying;
He had a word to say;
And those words finally saved me.
I recite them every day.

"You ain't no Super Hero, son.;
No more so than I.
But you'll find that you have powers.
Have you ever known me lie?

Take a care for someone else,
Before each day goes by.
You'll find what's special 'bout yourself;
That's when you'll really fly.

Stand by your woman
When she risks her life in birth.
Stand by your Mom and Dad
When they depart this Earth.

Stand by your Country
But make peace when you can.
You'll never fly; but 'til you die,
You'll be a super Man."

I straightened up. I finished school;
Got a job and met a gal.
Nothing special: small house, small kids, big truck;
A dog whom we call, "Hal – *on Earth* ."

With gratitude and wonder,
I watch my children grow.
And when they fail to fly, they cry;
I tell them what I know:

"You ain't no Super Hero, gal,
No more so than I am;
When you can't do the very best,
You do the best you can.
(*Spoken*) That's what it is to be a human.
. . . . . What it is to be a super Woman."

I was playing Super Hero,
Jumping off my Grandma's porch.

Goodnight, Daddy.
Thanks, Dad.
We love you, Daddy!
Look, Daddy, I can fly!

DINER
Robert E. McGill

My Boondock's home-style DINER
Was the center of our town.
More deals were made there
Than City Hall would ever see go down.

That's where George Webb proposed to Emily.
At the Graduation Dinner on Prom night.
Jim went broken-hearted jealous crazy;
They broke some teeth and tables.
        (*Spoken*) It was a memorable fight.

Everybody ate there, if not twice, least once a day:
Best looking waitresses you've ever seen.
Coffee at sunrise; delicious homemade pies;
And most everything you could think of in between.

The food was more than memorable;
And memories were made.
We learned as much there as in school
From Kindergarten through twelfth grade.

I went back there several years ago;
Thought I'd step inside.
"The usual?" asked Carly Rose,
From my favorite table's side.

She'd aged, but her smile was the same
Ole sly, shy c'mon as it was back in the day.
We talked of those who' died, who'd married,
Of those who left and those who stayed.

When I left, we knew we'd never meet again.
Carly-Rose kissed me on the lips.
"I'll doggy bag what's left for you." She said.
"Don't come back unless you leave me a good tip!"
        (*Spoken*) You can be sure I did.

I've heard it said, "you can't go home again."
I did; and I was welcomed in
As if I'd arrived in Heaven
Completely free of sin.

If you go looking for an earlier you,
Search out that part, the heart that's remained true.
Most everything will have changed and rearranged
Except the part that's always part of you.

WE THE PEOPLE
Robert E. McGill

 A young girl hop-scotches - skips and dodges - 'cross the street.
She's the earliest of birds, first browser,
At a neighborhood yard sale. It's just past dawn;
The dew's still on the lawn. It'll be gone
Before it gets a chance to damp her dancing feet.

She yearns to plunder through this splendid panoply.
Who knows what treasures may be found, lying around,
That only her well-trained eye will see
Among the hum-drum discards of a stranger's family?

She anticipates discovery of an unexpected treat;
So, she dawdles, savoring, delaying her arrival;
For expectation is as sweet as finding something wonderful
for half a dollar. If you *bargain*, she has learned,
And play for time, the prize's price grows smaller.
At yard sales, a treasure can be had for just a dime.

She dreams a wish she never speaks of openly.
She's heard of stories; she believes they're true.
Perhaps, she'll find stacked up and backwards,
Against a not-quite-stable table, a dreary portrait painting
Of someone, that once upon a time, somebody loved;
And tucked inside its age-stained, paper backing will be a copy of
Thomas Jefferson's Declaration of Independence.
And she dreams she'll get it for a buck or fifty cents; maybe for free.
And she dreams of independence. And she dreams of being free.

But she'll settle for a special kind of paperweight,
Any small thing – a fountain pen – that inked
Some other, admittedly less famous, declaration.
She is a seeker of imagination's talismans;
She will skip away enhanced and satisfied,
Out, maybe a buck or two and change. She's changed,
Possessed with newfound relics of antiquity,
Illuminated and transfigured with epiphany,
She knows that mystery surrounds us; and she's
Found her happiness in the pursuit of mystery.

There's a man inside the first garage that she visits.
He looks tired, more than old; and so does what he's sorting through:
Oil paintings. Cheap frames, muddled colors, still, worth investigating.
She finds one that suggests it might just be worthwhile;
But the price tag is beyond her meager budget by a mile.
The man sees her flinch of disappointment.

"I'll tell you *what*." he says," Pick out something more your style.
I guarantee, I'll give you a good deal, all but for free."
She says, "I'll tell *you* what." She's not rude.
She's market-shrewd; just establishing her territory.

She inquires, "Would you hold onto this for me awhile?"
Immediately she knows the answer from his weary smile.
"I'm having a sale here. I'm getting *rid* of things
Why would it occur to you that I'd 'hold onto' anything? No can do.
I know! Don't tell me. I know you're looking for The Declaration."
She is amazed; and then absorbs a lesson from the *Agora*:
Manipulative myths abound. Old timers and real pros know all the tales.
She might as well have said, "Do you have the Holy Grail on sale?

She asks, "How much you want?"
He says, "Read the tag and weep." This isn't his first Rodeo.
He knows her kind. He's not asleep.
"Ten dollars?" The girl is devastated. All she has
Is her hard-earned, paper-route six bucks.
Then she remembers her Dad gave her a dollar
When he dropped her off; then went for coffee down at 7/ll.
He always chipped in and wished her luck. She'll need it
To bargain this shrewd dude down to seven.

The man and she agree that *if* she purchases the painting,
She owns all of its contents, completely.
Unless, of course, the painting hides a copy of the Declaration,
In which case they will split the profits.
"How about 70/30?" she offers. 80/20 would have been too rash.
He shrugs and agrees. Doesn't Matter!
She still doesn't have the cash!

"How much did you say?" She asks again. He says, "A sawbuck.
Ten bucks, as is so very clearly printed on the sign."
The lass knows well she's broken the first rule of the bazaar.
She has allowed the seller to know what her true desires are.
He knows she *wants* that painting. Now he holds all the cards.
"What's it a painting of?" She's tap-dancing, buying time.
"Is it what they call, "A Still Life?"
He says, "It's clearly a sun-set. Well, maybe a sunrise?"
She feigns distain. He says, "Let me check it with the wife."

     He turns and yells upstairs,
     "MILLIE, SOMEONE WANTS TO BUY A PAINTING!"
         "Which one?"
            "THE YELLOW ONE!"
            "How much?"
                "SHE HASN'T MADE AN OFFER."
                  "Wait. I'm coming down. Ask her to stay."

     "MILLIE, I THINK IT'S NOT SO MUCH YELLOW AS IT'S BROWN."
        "Oh, *that* one. talk 'er down; if you can't, give it away."

Now he's not got a leg to stand on.
He says, "I stand amazed and know not what to say."[v]
He presents her with the painting as if awarding The Crown Jewels.
What about our deal?" She asks.
He says, "Possession rules. Deal's off, sister. Good luck!"
"Thanks so much, Mister!" On legs as thin as stilts,
She lilts, hop-scotching her way, away.

Other buyers are approaching now;
She'd like to browse some more;
But as she totes the painting to the car;
She decides, "Open it now! Time to explore!"
She reminds herself the odds are just impossible,
And not to get her hopes the least bit high.

She pries away old staples, bent and tiny, rusty nails.
She peels away the crinkly, crumbling paper backing;
Behold! A folded vellum manuscript. The document is frail.
With reverence, she carefully unfolds one corner.

The bells begin to peal In Paul Revere's Old North Church Steeple.
In stylish script, three words appear,
Penned in Thomas Jefferson's fine hand,
Writ large and clear: *WE THE PEOPLE*,

"Dad," she says, "Here's your dollar back."
"Bring you luck?" She nods, "I guess."
She has no idea what's in store; but she won't need
A paper-route or borrowed dollars anymore.

"I want to go to college, Dad. Don't worry. I'll pay for."

---

[v] Shakespeare, William. A MIDSUMMER NIGHT'S DREAM. Act II, scene iii

WELCOME AS THE SPRING IS TO THE EARTH
Robert E. McGill

Hey, Mister Greyhound Man, just pop the latch.
I'll fetch her luggage; you can just sit still.
Hi! Honey! Jump in the car; stay warm.
Give me a hug? You're looking fit to kill.

If you're starving, we can stop? No?
Well, there's stuff back at the place.
How was your trip? You made good time.
Girl, it's great to see your face.

    Lonely's when the only company you keep,
    Is a half pint of whisky to help you to sleep.
    Lonely's a desert as empty as can be.
    Lonely's a dead man walking, until you came home to me.

How 'bout dinner and a movie;
Or stay home and watch TV?
Of course, you can crash early.
God, I'm nervous. Can't you see?

I'll take the couch. I got work early.
You sleep-in, my morning star.
There are clean sheets on our bed . . .
Well you remember where things are.

    Lonely's when the only company you keep,
    Is a half pint of whisky to help you to sleep.
    Lonely's a desert as empty as can be.
    Lonely's a dead man walking, until you came home to me.

Nothing's changed or rearranged.
Not as neat as it should be.
We've a good home in need of some repair.
Nothing we can't fix, if you agree.

I don't know why you left me.
But it taught me how much you're worth.
I know now you're home where you belong.
And "welcome as the spring is to the earth."

    (Shakespeare THE WINTER'S TALE Act V, Scene ii)

CHAPTER 5:

LOVE SONGS: *Sad, Glad & Mostly In-Between*

WHY ARE WE WASTING BOTH OUR LIVES?
Robert E. McGill

A home's a place where love should thrive;
Where every dream should come alive;
Not where bedrooms are taboo;
And my presence sickens you;
And the silence cuts like knives.

Why are we wasting both our lives?
When love dies nothing else survives.
God knows I've tried and tried;
But I've failed you, and I've lied.
Why are we wasting both our lives?

Let's cut the ties and just run free;
Go discover you and I'll discover me.
Put an end to this illusion.
Please, can't we end the agony?

I had felt these things so long;
Then one day when things went wrong,
You hugged and took me by the hand;
And I came to understand
      You are my soul's abiding song

Why aren't we *tasting* both our lives?
Let's not waste time till death arrives.
Won't you once more be my wife?
We'll celebrate a brand-new life.
If not, may your heart be healed and thrive.

     REPRISE: A home's a place where love should thrive.

A SONG FOR CATHERINE
Robert E. McGill

She went by Cathy; I called her Catherine:
Sky-blue eyes and hair of saffron.
A luminescent beauty shown
Around her, and your heart found home.
     She is the lightest soul I've ever known.

Her heart darted: a lake-skipping pebble.
Brave wave-rider; bit of a rebel.
It was herself she'd thrown,
Fearless of the wave's crest's foam.
     She is the lightest soul I've ever known.

        If you have a Catherine to nuzzle,
        Then life's a *not*-cross word puzzle.
        Catherine says, "No need to guess.
        To life and love the answer's always 'YES!'"

Now if I had to make a list of qualities she missed,
First would be her fine, Italian red-wine lips.
They'd not refuse, resist or turn down a kiss;
Nor could they turn down in a frown
     listen to her grin. you'll hear bliss resound.
       (*spoken*) she wears laughter like a gown.

Oh, she could suffer. Of course, she suffered;
But Catherine was much tougher.
She took - from her sorrows - wisdom;
And we watched, like a rising, shining sun,
     The most generous of artists she'd become.

        If I had to make a list of
        All the things I missed of
        Doing enough to make her my own,
        First, I took her light; but mine I kept shut down.

        She forgave me that and taught me
        Life is ecstasy; and all we ought be
        Good at is (*can be spoken*) saying, "Yes !" to joy
        And love and one another

I let her go but don't regret her
Finding someone so much better.
No one could alone possess her.
Catharine's the whole world's to own.
        She is the lightest soul I've ever known.

BACK IN THE DAY
Robert E. McGill

Back in the day, when I was still in love with you,
Things were better; Rain was wetter,
Life was easier; bacon was greasier
Back in the day, when I was still in love with you.

Back in the day, Oh! I was so in love with you;
I didn't want to sleep. I had to be on hand
To witness the next miracle you'd do,
Back in the day, when I was still in love with you.

One day, back in the day, I heard you say,
"People fall out of love. It happens all the time."
You said it casually, so coldly smart;
It seared my soul and burned into my mind.
(*Spoken*) When it proved true it broke my heart.

"Love is momentary as a sound;
Swift as a shadow, short as any dream's illusion;
Brief as the lightning in the coal-eyed night.
So quick, bright things come to confusion."

(Shakespeare. MSND. Act I, scene ii)

NOT TRUE!

Back in the day, when I was still in love with you,
Is just a tick of time or so ago – no more than two.
Tomorrow too, my love will still and always be as new
As it was back in the day, when I was still in love you.
(*Spoken*) AND I AM STILL IN LOVE WITH YOU!

BEFORE I KNEW YOUR NAME

Robert E. McGill

I'm wonderin' 'bout our Grand-kids to be.
I guess that puts me out over my skis.
I'm <u>not</u> wondering how long I'm gonna love you.
I'd guess at best, when laid to rest, a few eternities.

I'm wondering too, since I saw you,
How nothing's gonna be the same.
I'm wondering, how to tell you that I love you,
When – as for now - I don't yet know your name?

You crashed this barroom - don't you agree? -
Splashing beauty like a **sur**prise tsunami.
You gave the bartender a wave. I asked him to save
You a place here at the bar, right next to me.

I figure if I slip him five/ten dollars,
I'll up my odds of winning love's sweet game.
I'd like him to introduce us, he knows us both;
But – as of yet - I still don't know your name.

       Falling in love at first sight
       Is the stuff of tragedy.
       There are thousands of broken hearts
       That will gladly – sadly – agree.

       We're warned about rash passion,
       And the thrall of chemistry.
       We're told we'll end up one of those fish
       Who are the "others" in the sea.

       There are sharp rocks beneath the waves
       Upon the lakes of love we choose to dive.
       You can wade in, and live; or plunge headfirst.
       If you survive, you'll finally be alive.

So, I'll sit here until you notice me.
Then we'll be introduced; I'll know your name.
I'm thinking our prospects are looking great.
What I feel is real. Hope you feel the same.

*(**NOTE***) Here's an "interruption," almost as if we were listening to their spiritual communication, a telepathy, envisioning the future. Can be done by solo singer; or, if a female voice is available, she takes lines as noted:* **S.**

May I have this dance, my Lady?
S May I waltz with you tonight?
May we dance in love and marriage,
S Until we say our last 'Goodnight'?

You are love eternal, beauty, wisdom, grace,
S All of these, your virtues, wrapped in fame.
My luminescent, transcendent angel.
BOTH: I loved you so before I even knew your name.

Our earthly love one day will pass away.
But we'll hook up after our dying day. (*Spoken*) Right away!
Then I'll get back to loving you more than I did before
After forever after, and then forevermore.

Falling in love at first sight
Is the stuff of tragedy.
There are thousands of broken hearts
That will gladly – sadly – agree.

We're warned about rash passion,
And the thrall of chemistry.
We're told we'll end up one of those fish
Who are the "others" in the sea.

There are sharp rocks beneath the surfaces
Of the lakes of love we choose to dive.
You can wade in cautiously; and you will live;
Or plunge and die or plunge and come alive.

And to the end of time I will proclaim
I loved you long before I knew your name.

I LOVE YOU MORE THAN COFFEE
Robert E. McGill

I love you more than coffee,
When the morning work's half through.
I love you more than long-neck beers,
When I come home to you.

I love you, when we go to bed,
And make love all night long;
Then sleep to wake and love again,
Beneath the breaking dawn.

I love you more than laughter;
More than camping 'neath the moon.
More than mountains and the oceans
Tell us, "Life ends way too soon."

Sometime, before eternity,
We'll know what life is for;
But to know how much I love you
Will take eternity and more.

So, for now, knowing how I love my brew,
Know that, more than coffee, I love you.

(*reprise – if desired*) I love you more than coffee.

I NEVER KNEW HER NAME
Robert E. McGill

Good evening, Ma'am. How are you?
Folks call me, Cookie. May I know your name?
I understand. I apologize.
It's just you look the same as . . .

Just wondering, do you have a twin?
No. Well, thanks. That'll have to do.
Oh? Why do I want to know?
You buy the next round; I'll tell you.

For the last year and a half or so
This girl who looked like you,
Would sit just where you're sitting;
And she'd grant me a dance or two.

 She'd poke me if I held her too tight.
I'd see her home; but never spent the night.
I counted her a friend. We talked the same.
Though I'm ashamed to tell you, I never knew her name.

        This was most every Friday night,
        Until about a month ago;
        Then she didn't come one night.
        (*Spoken*) A couple weeks went by
        And still she didn't show.

I drove by her house; but it was empty.
Don't know what became of her;
but you look the same as her,
Maybe just a bit prettier

She said, "No, she's prettier than me,
Though I appreciate your choice to disagree.
Last time I saw her she asked me if I would
Do her a favor, if I'd be so good.

She wanted me to come here and meet you.
Tell you how much she treasured what the two of you
Created and how you seemed to give a damn,
Instead of "Wham/Bam! Thank you, Ma'am!"

You befriended her lonely heart.
It was a shame, she said, "You never knew her name."
She told me, if I found you, by some chance,
I should say, "Hi!" and ask you for a dance

And you can hold me too tight,
If you want to take the chance.
We'll see if anything's the same.
If so, I just may let you know my name.

IF YOU DON'T MIND, I'LL LEAVE MY HEART BEHIND
Robert E. McGill

I'm all packed up, I'm good to go.
Ten minutes more and I'll be on my way.
If there's anything that I forgot
I'll pick it up, come Saturday.

Just one more thing. Is there a place
Only you and I could ever find,
A secret, special, precious space,
Where I could leave my heart behind?

    I need a place to leave my heart behind.
    There's no use for it I'll ever find.
    It's broken. Maybe it'll heal in time. (*Spoken*) For now
    I need a place to leave my heart behind.

You keep the wedding crockery.
No use breaking up those gifts.
You keep the Stereo and T.V.
We've broken up enough sets as it is.
    (*Spoken*) I'll commandeer that old microwave,
And take a lamp with me.

I'll claim a stray from the ASPCA,
A mutt to make me take a walk.
Help me get through it if I get 'round to it.
He'll listen when I need to talk.

    I had to be deaf dumb and blind to let you go.
    There was plenty time to make you mine.
    I'll forever have you on my mind; (*Spoken*) For now
    I need a place to leave my heart behind

REPRISE

(*Sprechtsingen*)   I need a place to leave my heart behind
<u>**or**</u>
I'm all packed up I'm good to go

MY LADY, WILL YOU BE MY PARTNER FOR A DANCE?
Robert E. McGill

Every Friday night you walk into our favorite local bar.
You make the place a better place by far.
 When you're here, we're better than we are on our own.
When you're around, we're surrounded; nobody feels alone.
You make us all walk taller than we knew that we could walk.
I know I'll get at least once dance and the chance to talk.

    CHORUS
    You are my star; You share your warmth and light.
    You make us shine far brighter than we might.
    You show us how to care for someone else;
    You teach us how to love beyond ourselves.
    I love that in you, and I love you that way too.
    I think it's way past time that you knew.

Trouble is I'm never quite sure if you're here with or without.
Night out with the girls? Is there a guy lurking about?
And I'm always thinking when you say, "Goodbye."
Why don't I ask if I might see you home?
But my heart fumbles; and I mumble, "See ya, soon;"
And you look at me like I'm some sort of goon.

    CHORUS
    You are my star; You share your warmth and light.
    You make us shine far brighter than we might.
    You show us how to care for someone else;
    You teach us how to love beyond ourselves.
    I love that in you, and I love you that way too.
    I think it's way past time that you knew.

If I asked you out, would you check your I phone
For an alibi and decline; Or would you say
I've been waiting. you sure took your sweet time?
What would you say, if I asked you to be mine;
Would you hesitate or say, "Hey! Any time!
I sit here silent as a clam, fool that I'm.

CHORUS
You are my star; You share your warmth and light.
You make us shine far brighter than we might.
You show us how to care for someone else;
You teach us how to love beyond ourselves.
I love that in you, and I love you that way too.
I think it's way past time that you knew.

 Some night when you don't show I'll ask after you.
Someone will say, "Oh, I thought you knew.
She told me I should tell you She met somebody new;
But that she'd always be a little bit in love with you.
That does it! This will not stand! Fine! I'll take my chance.
My Lady, will you be my partner for a dance?

WIDOW WOMAN
Robert E. McGill

There's a Widow Woman
Lives close to me; yet far.
Prettier than all the dreams
You dream, when wishing on astar.

Cancer and whiskey took her men.
Neither death did she deserve.
She's earned her right to solitude.
She keeps her passions in reserve.

> The evening stars are melting, Widow Woman.
> The day's half done; and you're alone.
> Wish upon a star to bar
> That angry venom from your bed.
> Your bitterness will turn your heart to stone;
> And leave you dead.

I would wake beside you, Woman,
When the darkness steals the light;
When one human needs another
To dance away the fright.

Oh, lonely, Widow Woman,
I would love to be your spouse!
Won't you let me introduce myself?
Life's not an empty house.

> The evening stars are melting, Widow Woman.
> The day's half done; and you're alone.
> Wish upon a star to bar
> That angry venom from your bed.
> Your bitterness will turn your heart to stone;
> And leave you dead

(*Spoken*) Woman,
 Know, when you silently pass by,
I stand watch for you;
And if you'd take my heart in hand,
I'd watch over all you do.

PUSH COMES TO SHOVE
Robert E. McGill

When you've walked through poison ivy,
You've gotta scratch that itch;
When your pickup truck won't start up,
You gotta fix that glitch.

And when, one day, you meet *that* gal,
One look; push comes to shove.
You stand no chance against romance;
You've gotta fall in love.

    You can hide your heart from sight;
    Stow it someplace hard to find.
    They say that love can't see; (*Spoken*) Maybe;
    She still will rob you blind.

Think hating her, not dating her,
Might work? Don't be a dope.
You can't push back the shove of love.
You're on a slippery slope.

When you can't stop smiling;
Cuz she's all you're thinking of,
Then take her; better make her yours.
It's time you fell in love.

    You can hide your heart from sight;
    Stow it someplace hard to find.
    They say that love can't see; (*Spoken*) Maybe;
    She still will rob you blind.

You're lucky to have found her.
Not everyone's so blessed.
Some will never win the prize
On love's long, lonely quest.

You've been a long time lonely;
Now Love's push has come to shove.
Fall like the leaves in autumn do.
Hey, shoved lover, fall in love.

CHAPTER 6:

***PATRIOTIC
PIUS
PROTEST***

COUNTRY MEADOW SYMPHONY

Robert E. McGill

When the Southern Summer pavement's heat
Burns my boots and Bar-B-Ques my feet,
There's a place in my imagination where I go.
I walk barefoot through a Country Boy's meadow.

I'll hold my hand out. Take it! See, you're here.
I beckon and a country meadow will appear.
My love, come barefoot. Dare share my mystery.
"Lend me your ears;"[vi] You'll hear a country meadow symphony

In a country meadow, you'd think quiet would abound.
Just the opposite! There are waterfalls of sound.
Insects sing to crickets' wings; Listen! Buzzing, chirping, croaking.
Makes you wonder what this country orchestra is smoking.

    What's best about the country is the country:
    God's green earth: mud you can scrunch between your toes.
    Listen in the roaring silence for all the songs creation sings.
    Here are "books in running brooks;' Here are "tongues in trees."[vii]
    Sermons in stones and good in everything."[viii]
    What's best about the country is the country.
        (*Spoken*) A country meadow's where you plant your soul to have it grow.

Once found, a sound is blown every which way.
From some far-flung, farm acre, a chorus wafts our way.
It's all of Old Macdonald's Barn-Yard crew!
"Here a heifer, there a rooster; everywhere a ewe or two."
    (*Spoken*) E- I, E- I, O! or, in this case, "Oh! You!"

Next field over, Cornstalk Mister whispers
To Sunflower Sister, softly, sweet and low.
His all but silent flirts; her rustling skirts
Speak secrets only butterflies can know.

Not even the best concert at the Grand Ole Opry
Could hold a candle to a country meadow's symphony.
It's even more fantastical than all
That classical *fol- de- rol* rapping at Carnegie Hall.

What's best about the country is the country:
God's green earth: mud you can scrunch between your toes.
Listen in the roaring silence for all the songs creation sings.
Here are "books in running brooks;' Here are "tongues in trees;
Sermons in stones and good in everything."[ix]
What's best about the country is the country.
A country meadow's where you plant your soul to have it grow.

Is your heart as quiet as the meadow?
Or is it noisy: Music everywhere you go?
Excuse me, if I have to raise my voice to say
"I love you" in that same noisy-quiet way.

Will you walk life's country meadow with me?
Take my ring. Say, "Yes?" I'm down on bended knee.
If we can imagine a country meadow's symphony,
Imagine all we'll feel for real, if you'll just marry me.
          (*Spoken*) Take my hand; and raise me up!
                    Meadow mud won't let go my knee!

[vi] Shakespeare, William. JULIUS CAESAR. Act II, scene iii
[vii] Shakespeare, William. AS YOU LIKE IT. Act II, scene i
[viii] Shakespeare, William. AS YOU LIKE IT. Act II, scene i
[viii] Shakespeare, William, AS YOU LIKE IT. Act II, scene i

PAINT MADE IN THE U.S.A.
Robert E. McGill

Take my hand, my friend. I understand if you won't.
Some of your best friends don't look quite like me.
Some of my best friends don't look a lot like you.
Just know I really care either way. Honestly, I do.

Just as sure as our Liberty Bell won't ever ring
Because it's broken, we're broken too. We've got to solve this thing.
Let's Abraham Linconize each other. You set me; I'll set you free.
Free from our stereotyped atrocities.

No one should die because they're wearing hoodies.
No one should die because they're a Jew.
No one should ever die at hatred's hands;
But who's gonna stop it, if not me and you?

Pour the colors out, all together, black and white,
Brown, yellow, native red and as many shades
Beyond those that we can see.
What we got? A color without a name.
NO color! And that makes us all the same.
God be thanked for our diversity! I say
That's how America plays its game.
We The People wear a paint made only IN THE U.S.A.

There're at least a hundred things on which we'll disagree;
But that's what's at the heart of preserving our democracy.
        FREEDOM OF EXPRESSION!
            RESPECT! and
                SAFETY GUARANTEED!

Take my hand, man. Let's celebrate our liberty.
Let's not forget how far we've come and who
Laid down their lives to keep the dream alive.
What would Martin, what would Bobby do?

Take my hand, brother, that's what we must do.
Let go of hate. Bury what our fathers suffered through.
Let their suffering empower me and you
To, Yes! Of course, Amend! But more importantly transcend
The past and create something new. Alone, neither of us knows what to do.

Take my hand. Together there's nothing we can't do.

GOLD STAR
Robert E. McGill

There is a Gold Star family.
They live across the street.
They're neighbors; but we've never met.
Now there's one we'll never meet.

They flew a flag with one Blue Star,
For their patriot at war across the ocean.
Today they changed that blue star to a Gold Star.
Their soldier child has paid their last full measure of devotion.

War is a necessary evil
That extracts a horrid cost:
If freedom is to triumph,
Precious children must be lost.

But what is found and ever treasured
Is their sacrifice and bravery;
And a grateful nation's eternal thanks
To those who kept us free.
       (*Spoken*) May those who go, come safely home to you;
       And may their Star remain forever Blue.

          "Oh, beautiful for heroes proved
          In liberating strife,
          Who more than self their country loved;
          And mercy more than life.
             America, America,
             God shed his grace on thee;
             And crown they good with brotherhood,
             From sea to shining sea."   (AMERICA, THE BEAUTIFUL)

Next time you see a soldier,
Share a word with her or him.
Don't just thank them for their service.
Take time to ask them where they've been.

They may not wish – or be able– to tell you all they've done.
Remember, they have earned your honor and your praise.
They don't owe more than that to anyone.
       (*Spoken*) May their Blue Star not turn to Gold
Until they've lived out their allotted days.

ONLY OKLAHOMA

Robert E. McGill
With credit to Bubba Keltch

I'm cruising south on US 35.
I'm doing 50 miles per hour slow.
I'm enjoying heeding the speed limit.
I'm already where I want to go.
Just crossed the Oklahoma State Line's
"WELCOME" sign a mile or so ago.

The sunset paints a gentle, pastel portrait:
A southern lady's sweet "Good Night, Y'all."
The landscape might as well be painted scenery.
Nothing ever changes here at all;
Not 'til some rogue hill from Missouri breaks
Through to start a whole new mural, wide and tall.

Oklahoma's beauty's wide and tall and flat;
So flat-out flat she can make you dizzy
With the notion the horizon is the ocean.
From our front porches we can see the sea.
If you believe the earth is flat
     (*Spoken*) And there's nothing' wrong with that.
Then Oklahoma's where you ought to be.

     Oklahoma, I'm only just anotha Bubba,
     Looking for his only Oklahoma home.
     Open your arms and take me in, my Oklahoma?
     Tell me that I can come home again.
     "I have a faint, cold fear steals through my veins
     That almost freezes up the heat of life."[x]
     Will you still be the same, my Oklahoma?
     Momma? Best Friend? Daddy? Loving Wife?
        (*Spoken*: There's a dog, a brother and a sister too, whom I love more than life.)

I'm an entertainer by profession.
Aren't we all? I can pitch bull puckie with the best;
But here I hold a hundred acres in my keep;
And elbow deep in real cow-pie I find my rest.
You dasn't have to lie to Oklahoma.
Her acceptance speaks within me. I am blessed.

---

[x] Shakespeare, William. ROMEO AND JULIET. Act IV, scene ii

I'm blessed; the hunting and the fishing speak to me
Of what I've been and what I've yet to find.
No matter how much and many changes,
I'm only Oklahoma: harsh and kind.
          (*Spoken*) We are owed nothing.
What worth we make will surely be defined.
By how much love we choose to leave behind.

          Oklahoma, I'm only just anotha Bubba,
          Looking for his only Oklahoma home.
          Open your arms and take me in, my Oklahoma?
          Tell me that I can come home again.
          "I have a faint, cold fear steals through my veins
          That almost freezes up the heat of life." [xi]
          Will you still be the same, my Oklahoma?
          Momma? Best Friend? Daddy? Loving Wife?
                    (*Spoken*: There's a dog, a brother and sister too, whom I love more than life.)

[xi] Shakespeare, William. ROMEO AND JULIET. Act IV, scene ii

WHAT JESUS DOES.

Robert E. McGill

Don't you think He harbors animosity?
Don't you think He suffers guilt; cowers in shame?
Don't you think He rehearses vengeance
      (*spoken*) All in the Father's name?
Don't you think He savors His tormenter's pain?

Does He try to be like Jesus then?
Does he become more Godlike and remote?
No. He swallows his humanity
Like a fish bone, caught in his throat.

He forgives himself; embraces the mystery
Of our wretched human, wondrous states.
He learns to love his fellow man entirely:
Our sins, our soaring souls He celebrates.
      (*Spoken*: <u>He says,</u>) "A man may follow many a false trail,
      While he is on the path to finding me."

Don't you think He probably places a bet or two?
Don't you think, one night, He probably drinks too much?
We know he can be angry, often violent.
Don't you think, He hungers for a woman's touch?

So, next time you're moping, bitter, put-upon,
You're doing what Jesus does; but remember this.
He quits those wastes of precious life and time.
He banishes hatred forever with His kiss.

        Don't you think that He is less of God;
        And more like all of us?

YEARNING TO BE FREE
Robert E. McGill

William Shakespeare was alive, when first they came.
They came before New York Harbor had its name.
Long before the tall-torched lady lit their way,
They came from near and far away. They came;
And they became all that we are today:
America, America; the grand,
Our welcoming, demanding, generous land.

Some came to practice their religions;
Some came of all religion to be free.
Some came to hunt or work the land in blessed liberty.
Some, heading west, stopped here to rest;
Woke up, stayed the day, and never left.
Some came to dig the killer coal and grow their family.

They carried their possessions on their backs.
 And far more precious things than fit in sacks.
The soul's a roomy portmanteau to tote
memories of homelands they'll never be without
Always: faith, hope and charity; and . . . oh!
Song and dance, no doubt.

The covenant was simple: "Live your dream.
Use your talents. Use your muscle You'll succeed
Regardless of your color or your creed;
And your children will be better off than you."
America depends upon her children to uphold that guarantee.
It's time to wake, America. Your dreams are growing dark.
We're divided our differences are violent, and we feel
Our Liberty imperiled. Our country must be healed.

No one owns America. America owns us.
We claim our share by caring for her liberty.
When each and every one of us is treated equally.
America will have achieved her destiny.

All this depends on you and me
All children of the immigrant family
Take a stranger's hand in amity;
The healing has begun. Let's get this done.
Make it job one. It's our responsibility.

Take my hand and I'll take yours;
Then she'll take his and you take hers.
Soon enough we'll be America again; the grand:
Our welcoming, demanding, generous land.

THE GOOD LORD'S GROCERY STORE
Robert E. McGill

In the middle of the dark, despairing forest of my mind, I lost my way.
Whether I lived or died didn't matter either way.
I prayed for my salvation; and an angel came to say,
"I know a place that deals in grace;
It's never far from where you are, wherever you may be.
It's open 24/11 as are the gates of Heaven.
It has all you're looking for. Come along with me.
We're going shopping at the Good Lord's Grocery Store."

Just walk right in, start shopping.
You won't need a cart.
The goods you will acquire
Can be carried in your heart.

in the Breakfast section select your morning prayer
A little meditation can dispel a whole day's care.
Pick up a pint of human kindness – No! make that a quart; No! Make it four.
We always run out of that stuff just when we need some more.

Choose a sprig of sweet forgiveness and a stalk of sympathy;
A can or two of tenderness and heartfelt empathy.
In the spice aisle bring home something that might please you and me.
A six pack of wild laughter would seal the deal for me.

You may be disappointed that there's no real food for sale:
No poultry, no hamburger, no steak, no lobster tail.
We only deal in produce that's spiritually agrarian;
And, in full disclosure mode, God is a vegetarian.

There are precious vials of wisdom on the highest shelves of all;
But you must wait to savor them until your soul grows tall
Enough to reach them; and their price is often pain.
Just one to a customer, until you come again.

In Organic Nutrition pick up hours, one per day,
To spend with friends and family, communicate and play.
This can become addictive, so you'll want more time they say.
Come back for more. God's grocery store gives good times away

There's an ancient, outdoor market where you trade and barter love.
You bid, you bluff, you bargain and what you become aware of
Is that you make the greatest profit when you ask nothing and give everything
To serve your fellow man. You may proceed to checkout.
Go and do the best you can.

But there is no checkout counter. Remember, everything is free;
But the Angel who helped bagged your goods, totes your necessities
She says, "Don't ever try to lift more than you can.
Be humble. Call God's Grocery Store. We have a service plan.

Call in advance of trouble and order some assistance.
Get on your knees. Just say, "Please," Give up your resistance.
Back up promises with action: Faith, Hope and Charity.
Pass all of your love forward. Now, have a blessed day.

At the exit was a raffle stand; and the grand prize was you.
I have more love than money, but I bought a chance or two.
If I could win *that* lottery and have you back with me,
I'd never stop to have to shop at the Good Lord's Grocery.

If your hunger's intuition
Seeks out spiritual nutrition,
You'll have to stock your cupboards
With items never used before.
I all but live inside that place
It's run by my sister, Grace

    [**Shopper**, "And just who might you be?
    Clerk; "Full name's Ms. FAITH-HOPE CHARITY.

Now come with me
Just one block more
Past North 44,
Let's go shopping at God's Grocery store

UPON THE SEA OF GALILEE
Robert E. McGill

Simon Peter and the Lord's apostles
Set sail upon The Sea of Galilee;
Without any warning,
They faced a maelstrom at sea.

Against the waves they struggled manfully;
But there are storms that daunt the stoutest heart.
They floundered in the waves.
Their craft was torn apart.

As they sank, drowning in the tempest,
By the brilliant lightning strikes they could see
Christ, their Lord and Savior,
Walking towards them on the sea.

At His command the storm ceased instantly.
The Apostles found their craft newly made whole.
Even for those who would betray Him,
Jesus had saved their mortal souls.

We are all Christ's Apostles, sons and daughters.
When we fall a-drowning in our misery,
Christ will raise us up to walk on water
Upon the universal Sea of Galilee.

(*Spoken*) Where his sacrifice rescued all humanity.

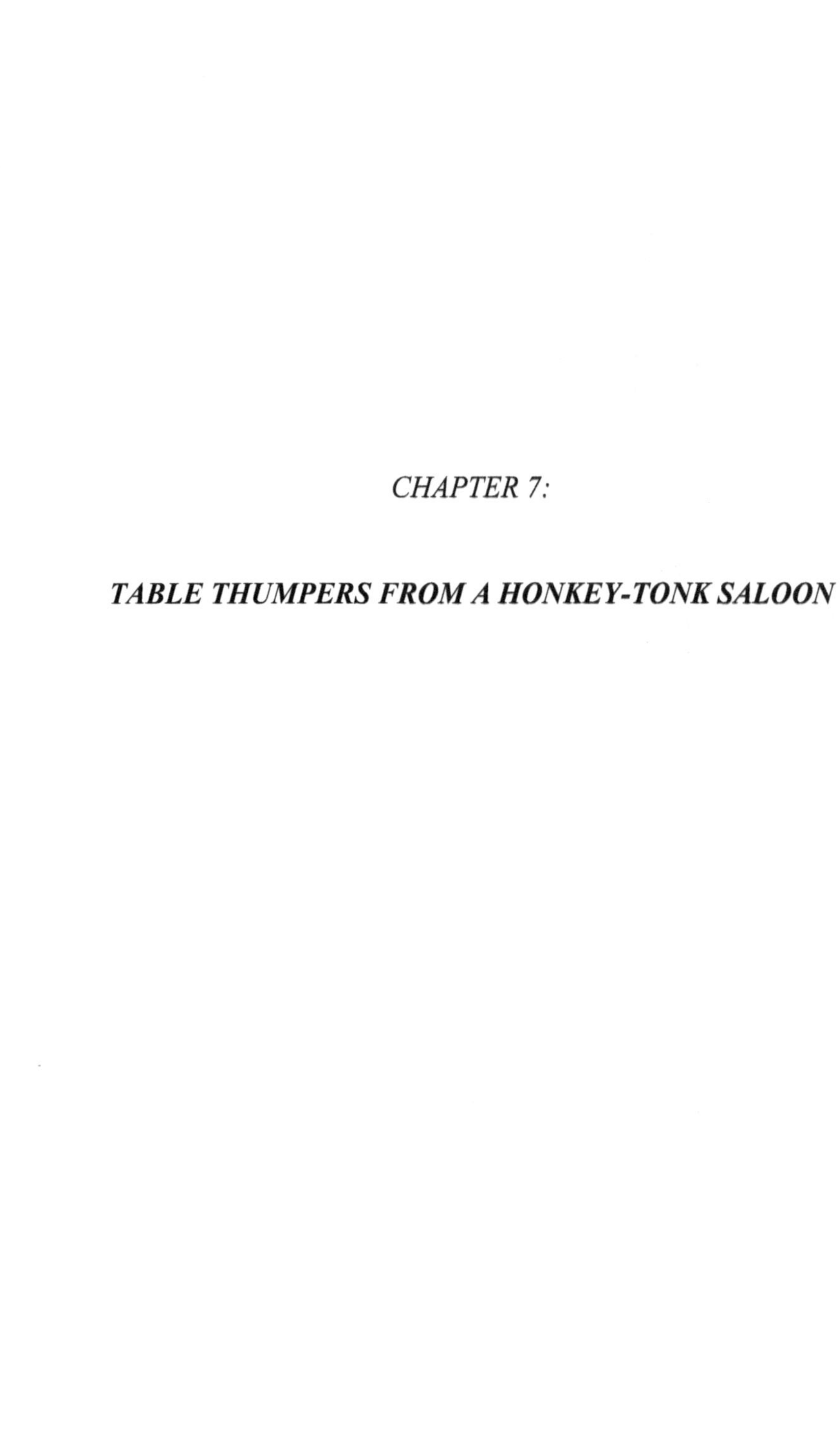

CHAPTER 7:

TABLE THUMPERS FROM A HONKEY-TONK SALOON

MAZIE, LET'S GET CRAZY!
Robert E. McGill

Mazie, let's get crazy!
Go get your dance boots on!
    Girl, grab your mini-skirt;
    And slap that denim on.
    Ditch those spikey high heels, girl;
    Forget your fancy gown.
(*Spoken*) Sometimes, the way you dress, I think I'm taking out your Mom!
Mazie, let's get crazy!
Go get your dance boots on!

Mazie, let's get crazy!
Go, get your dance boots on!
    Tell Dad we won't be long;
    Not *too* long (*beat& wink*) after dawn!
    He'll hear us, "Cock-a-Doodle-Do!"
    Right now, let's rock this town.
Mazie, let's get crazy!
Go, girl, get those dance boots on!

    My lady, get your cowgirl dance boots on!
    "Let's have ourselves one more gaudy night."(Antony & Cleopatra, III, xiii)
    We'll drive too fast and drink too much,
    We'll dance "two-step" and Line;
    If we're really fortunate, we'll get in a bar fight!
        (*Spoken*) That would be so fine.

    We'll do all the things an Oklahoma, small town Friday night
    Can offer you to do. We'll go for them. Both of them. Sad but true.
    What's truer is, I'm never blue when you're around.
    You be my mare; I'll be your stallion; and it's our time
    Too lend some horsepower to this One-horse-town. *AND*
(*Spoken*) I promise you! I do! that before this night is over, you'll be mine!

We'll get a buzz, get silly
At a bar called, MY BROTHER BILL'S
    GOT A STILL ON A HILL:
    Truly frightening lightning.
    If one sip won't kill ya;
    The second one damn will.

(**Performance note**: *"My brother Bill's Got a still on a hill." could* be sung to the melody of this old, campfire classic.

For dinner let's investigate
a new place: THE HYENA
    The name is rude; but they
    Traffic in African food.
    And if you want to go tribal
    You can dine in the nude . . .
        (*Spoken*) NO! Don't slap me, Maizy! I'm just kidding, being crazy.
        We can do Macdonald's, should you choose.
        'cept, remember, you thirsty wench, they don't serve booze.

We'll do some dancing, Mazie
 Two-Step; Polka, even a waltz.
    I'll slow dance and romance you,
    If you'll snuggle up real close.
    I'm crazy for you, Mazie.
    Won't you slip those dance boots off?

    My lady, crazy Mazie, get your cowgirl dance boots on!
    "Let's have ourselves one more gaudy night."
    We'll drive too fast and drink too much,
    We'll dance "two-step" and Line;
    If we're *really* fortunate, we'll get in a bar fight!
        (*Spoken*) That would be so fine.

    We'll do all the things an Oklahoma, small town Friday night
    Can offer you to do. We'll go for them. *Both* of them. Sad but true!
    What's truer is, I'm never blue when you're around.
    You be my mare; I'll be your stallion. And it's our time to
    Lend some horsepower to this 'One-horse-town;' AND
(*Spoken*) I promise you! I do! that before this night is over, you'll be mine!

Then we'll cruise on over to
"AND THE NIGHT GOES ON" saloon.
    We'll drop by, hear this guy,
    Kasey. They say he plays
    a hot guitar; and sings a decent tune.
    "Play it again," Kasey Yeargain.
        (*Spoken*) Last call. We'll always have
        Rick's Café Americain

Time to say goodnight, Mazie.
Mazie, get in the car.
>It's over here. I know
>You know. I know you knew. Don't fuss.
>You said, it was, "over here,"
>When you were over there . . . where . . . it once was.

>(**Performance note:** the first two lines of the following verse "*could*" be sung
> to the tune of the Irish ballad, "I'LL TAKE YOU HOME AGAIN, KATHLEEN.")

I'll take you home again, Mazie
Beneath an Oklahoma morning sky.
>We got crazy, Mazie
>I'm more than satisfied.
>Keep those dance boots dancing;
>One day You're gonna be my bride.

>>My lady, get your cowgirl dance boots on.
>>Let's have ourselves one more gaudy night.
>>We'll drive too fast and drink too much,
>>We'll dance "two-step" and Line;
>>If we're *really* fortunate, we'll get in a bar fight!
>>>(*Spoken*) That would be so fine.

>>We'll do all the things an Oklahoma, small town Friday night
>>Can offer you to do. We'll go for them. Both of them. Sad but true.
>>What's truer is, I'm never blue when you're around.
>>You be my mare; I'll be your stallion. And it's our time
>>To lend some horsepower to this 'One-horse-town. AND
(*Spoken*) I promise you! I do! that before this night is over, you'll be mine!

FOOTBALL LOVE

Robert E. McGill

Sitting in the stands, you take my hand;
My heart sings louder than the marching band.
You smile; and jets fly by, in the missing man formation.
I'm the fool gone missing, lost in adoration.

Girl, I've come to love you more than football;
And I love football more than I love life.
If I should win the coin of marriage toss,
(*Announcer*) I CHOOSE TO RECEIVE (*pause one beat*) YOU!
    (*Spoken*) - *If you'd have me* – as my wife.

    CHORUS
    Football love is never boring,
    Not when there's lots of scoring.
    You and I will scrimmage night and day.
    (*Announcer voice*) *"SHE MAKES HER FAVORITE PLAY!*
    HE'S THERE! HE INTERCEPTS!" Chris Berman says,
    "HE . . COULD . . GO . . ALL . . THE . . WAY!"

We'll suit up for our scrimmage every night.
We'll play smash-mouth with our lips and kisses.
You'll hike up your skirt; a razzle-dazzle, trick-play never hurt.
Football Love's a contact sport. Making love's what bliss is.

You won't catch me drawing a penalty for delay of game;
But my illegal use of hands will give you fits.
I'll play defensive back to get you in the sack;
And, I'll disrupt your backfield when I blitz.

    CHORUS
    Football love is never boring,
    Not when there's lots of scoring.
    You and I will scrimmage night and day.
    (*Announcer voice*) *"SHE MAKES HER FAVORITE PLAY!*
    HE'S THERE! HE INTERCEPTS!" Chris Berman says,
    "HE . . COULD . . GO . . ALL . . THE . . WAY!"

If I should chance to fumble as a lover,
We'll discover how your arms recover me.
We could end up locked up in a tie; That's fine.
We both win if we get to play some overtime.

Girl, I've come to love you more than football;
And you mustn't take that lightly.
I love football one, whole-awful lot;
But when you came along; I soon forgot

    CHORUS
    Football love is never boring,
    Not when there's lots of scoring.
    You and I will scrimmage night and day.
    (*Announcer voice*) *"SHE MAKES HER FAVORITE PLAY!*
    HE'S THERE! HE INTERCEPTS!" Chris Berman says,
    "HE . . COULD . . GO . . ALL . . THE . . WAY!"

PERFORMANCE NOTE: Lots of opportunity here for the performer to encourage the audience to join in on the chant, "HE . . COULD . . GO . . ALL . . THE . . WAY!"

GANGSTA' GAL
Robert E. McGill

(*Narrator voice*) We interrupt our programming to bring you breaking news:
A GANGSTA' GAL, A MASTER THIEF, IS ON THE LOOSE!

She's a nemesis, and she is on the premises!
She's cool, she's sleek, she's smart.
She's armed – and legged – and gorgeous;
And she's come to steal your heart.

(*Narrator voice*) We interrupt our breaking news with this breaking alert:
SHE'S A MASTER OF DISGUISE ALTHOUGH SHE'S PARTIAL TO A SKIRT.

She might be sitting lonely
At the far end of the bar;
Or she might be dancing by herself
In a corner of the floor.

She's a red-head, Irish, Pirate Queen
Who shuns sword or gun play.
When her Irish eyes are smiling,
Sure, they'll steal your heart away.

She's Kung-Fu and Karate trained.
Between your sneeze and her "God Bless you!",
She'll have your features re-arranged;
And break your spine in two.

    She's a complete professional;
    She'll treat you really nice.
    No one but your heart gets hurt
    When she says, "<u>Dis is a heist</u>*!*" *(Gangster voice)*

    She'll take all the love you carry,
    Just as she'll take your cash;
    And leave your broken wallet
    Of a heart out back in the trash.
    (*Spoken*) Don't fret!; She'll leave your credit cards and I.D.
    She's not that rash.

Her modus operandi is the flirt.
If she decides that you're her prize,
Don't matter if you freeze or run,
Your heart's gonna get hurt.

Until your tongue's tangled with hers,
You haven't yet been kissed.
That why she's *numero-uno*
On the FBI's, top ten, most *desirable* list.

When someone steals your money,
You mount a counterattack;
But when Gangsta' Gal steals your heart,
You might not want to get it back.
     (*Spoken*) Especially if the heist was fun;
      Done with a hint of sin, and not a gun.

     She's a complete professional.
     She'll treat you really nice.
     No one but your heart gets hurt
     When she says, "<u>Dis is a heist!</u>" *(Gangster voice)*

     She'll take all the love you carry,
     Just as she'll take your cash;
     And leave your broken wallet
     Of a heart out back in the trash.
       (*Spoken*) Don't fret! She'll leave your credit cards and I.D.
       She's not that rash.

She and I are partners in love and crime.
I'm her undercover lover. Thought you knew.
I let her flirt; she lets me too.
That's how we keep our romance shiny new.

To steal your heart, you'd be surprised
How for she'll go with you;
But don't let her get your hopes up;
To me she always will be true.

LET'S ALL FEEL SORRY FOR OURSELVES
Robert E. McGill

(*Mock dirge tempo. Lento*)
Tell you what: Let's all feel sorry for ourselves.
Have another beer and do some stinkin,' drinkin,' thinkin;'
Waste the chance to dance or have a real good time.
Just focus on, "I'm so this or that. I'm . . . I'm . . . I'm . . . I'm!"

(*Andante*)

HE: Debts, sick pets, lost bets, birthdays I forgot.
The right guy or gal I never met. Colds I got.
I have so much that I regret. I feel cursed eternally.
There's no sad soul on earth worse off than me.

SHE: My relationships all end way too early.
My lovers come (*beat*) - and go – (*beat*) prematurely.
I've gained a full-dress size. I'm getting burly.
They're calling me 'mature!' I should be 'girly!'
I've never given birth; but my girth grows like grass.
Do you think it's too big a thing? My AS . . .
. . . King you to agree with me?
There's no sad soul on earth worse off than me.

(*Lento*)

Tell you what: Let's all feel sorry for each other.
Get real maudlin, cry a little; hug one another.
I'm so sorry for your grief, Man, I am your brother.
You got it hard; you poor, suffering', bastard bugger.

(*Andante*)

SHE: I'm sorry for your loss, your awful boss, the cross
You carry. you've got a problem with the sauce.
HE: I'm in your shoes; I sing the blues for your bad news. I have great
sympathy.
HE & SHE: There's no sadder souls on earth worse than we three.
HE: Now let me tell you something about me.
(*Triumphant!. ☺)*

Tell you what: let's celebrate ourselves.
We've got this precious time to share. Let's play!
Put your cares and worries on the shelf.
We can feel sorry for ourselves some other day.
> Care for everyone as if they were your lover.
> You won't feel sorry for yourself when you're caring for another.

> (*Reprise*) There are no souls on earth happy as we.

(**NOTE**) *If desired, performer can recite, line by line, the last verse, inviting the audience to sing along with him after he reads each line. Or, if you'd like, here are the lyrics put to the tune of Beethoven's 9th, 4th movement: ODE TO JOY.)*

Tell you what: Let's celebrate this precious time we have to play.
Put off feeling sorry for ourselves until some other day.
Care for others like they were lovers;
Put all your worries on the shelf.
When you're caring for another,
You can't worry 'bout yourself.

(*Spoken*) *"Alle menschen werden Bruden!"*
"All men should be brothers!"
Thus did Beethoven write.
He stole from Friedrich Schiller;
But all men should be brothers.
And so: Goodnight!

LET'S HAVE SOME FUN TONIGHT

Robert E. McGill

HEARTACHE! Take a break! Enough of you!
I cannot abide you anymore.
Get up! Your butt's been sitting on my heart!
Go 'way! Get out! You can show yourself the door.

I've felt sorry for myself for far too long.
Long enough, that - if self-pity really worked -
By now I'd be possessed with happiness;
Not feeling like the world's loneliest jerk

    CHORUS
      Let's go and have some fun tonight!
      I'm feeling free; I'm feeling light.
      I'm prowling like a lonesome wolf;
      No shepherds are in sight.
      Lock up your daughters, Daddies!
      I'm huntin' fun tonight.

I'm going to the tavern
To have myself a beer.
Gonna find me some fine lady,
One who'll love to hold me near.

I'm going to the tavern
Where there's dancing; where there's song;
Where I can find love's smiley face.
Boot up and come along

    CHORUS
      Let's go and have some fun tonight!
      I'm feeling free; I'm feeling light.
      I'm prowling like a lonesome wolf;
      No shepherds are in sight.
      Lock up your daughters, Daddies!
      I'm huntin' fun tonight.

C'mon, let's go and have some fun tonight!
Nothin's so wrong that love can't make it right.
We can arm wrestle, two-step; or start a fight.
Make up and buy the guy a beer. "It's on me,
My new, best friend." Let's have some fun tonight!

Let's have some fun tonight!
After last call there's still a lot of night.
We'll drive too fast; and have a blast;
We'll make a damned good evening last;
And then go home patriotically!
    (*Sung to tune of National Anthem*: BY THE DAWN'S EARLY LIGHT.
Let's go have some fun tonight!

    CHORUS
      Let's go and have some fun tonight!
      I'm feeling free; I'm feeling light.
      I'm prowling like a lonesome wolf;
      No shepherds are in sight.
      Lock up your daughters, Daddies!
      I'm huntin' fun tonight.

Promise me we'll have some fun *tomorrow* night?
You'll know later-on this morning I was right.
You'll be fire-hose thirsty; and there'll be things you don't recall;
But – not to worry! - you'll soon regain full sight.
Hair of the dog will make you feel alright.
Bottom's up! Let's have some fun tonight!

SWEET KAY'S WEDDING NIGHT
Robert E. McGill

I was sitting up late grieving
For sweet Kay who lives next door.
She's a barmaid where I Tender
At a joint called *EAU DE FLEUR.*

We'd been best friends from the 'Get-Go;'
Though we never spent the night.
Now she'd gone and gotten married!
This was her wedding night. Tonight.

I didn't want to listen in;
I couldn't help but hear
Some stumbling and some muttering;
Then a silence that seemed queer.

I answered the knock upon my door;
There was the bride I'd missed:
My bar girl, sweet Kay, decked in bridal array.
I lifted her veil but *she* kissed.

She said, "Neighbor, a favor, *Voulez vou?*"
In return, I'll give a prize to you.
My Bridegroom's drunk. I'm still a maid.
But, Damn it! It's my wedding night;

>   (*Spoken*) And I'm sure as Hell gonna get laid.
>   Anyone who'll do will do; it might as well be you.

I know that a damsel in such deep distress
Might regret marriage vows that she'd ducked;
So I asked, "Don't you need to be certain?"
She said, "I just need to be . . .
                              . . . **"Lucked out!"** said I;
And gladly helped her consummate
The ritual and much more.
We never meet or speak again,
          'Cept at the *EAU DE FLEUR.*

PROBLEM WITH WOMEN

Robert E. McGill

CHORUS
I've got the world's worst problem with all women.
Don't get me wrong; I'm married happily.
It's that I've got this hang-dog look – or – *Effin* Something!
All kinds of women like to hit on me.

I must appear forsaken, isolated,
I must project vulnerability:
A tortured soul, bearing infinities of sorrow,
Complimented by my understated masculinity

I'm not buff, that young or handsome;
So, it must be something else these women see.
Whatever, it arouses more than their maternal care.
Although I wear my wedding ring, I stir up storms hormonally.

CHORUS
I've got the world's worst problem with all women.
Don't get me wrong; I'm married happily.
It's that I've got this hang-dog look – or – *Effin* Something!
All kinds of women like to hit on me.

I'm drinking solo and this mature 'Good-Looker'
Orders a dry martini in my Tex-Mex bar;
Snuggles up beside me and says, "It's a God-send.
You're my **_ONLY_** man. My search for love is at an end.
        I say, "I'm already taken, Lady. I'm so sorry."
        She says, "I'm desperate. Do you have a friend?"

This well-endowed, teen age Lolita
Cuddles up, way too close to me; she says,
Although she's no more than a mere child,
"How's about you and me do something wild?"
        I say, "You best go home to Daddy, girl. You're dangerous jailbait.
        She says, "I suppose that rules you out from being my prom date?"
                (*Spoken*) Damn straight!

I'm sipping a cold beer, minding my own business;
This hot-bod chick comes slinking up to me.
She says, "You're sad. I'll do what a companion should.
Take me home with you. I'll have you feeling good.
     "I can't do that." I say. "It would upset my wife and family."
     "Then chain them up in the front yard," she says, "until they're used to me."

    I've got the world's worst trouble with women.
    And, buddy, don't you wish that you were me?

CHAPTER 8:

DUETS FOR COUPLES OF ALL AGES

I NEVER SAID, "GOODBYE" TO YOU

Robert E. McGill

----------------------**P**<u>*resent Tense*</u>

BOTH:	So, here we are.
SHE:	How long's it been?
HE:	I'd say 20 years plus change.
SHE:	Say that again.
HE:	What? "Change?" I have.
SHE:	Me too. Time tanks.
HE:	You wouldn't know to look at you!
SHE:	Not quite.
HE:	You're right.
SHE:	Well, thanks!

-------------------------- <u>*Remebrance*</u>

BOTH	We shared a mystic harmony.
HE:	Our strides kept easy time.
BOTH	Our hands would find each other's;
SHE:	And our fingers closed the rhyme.
BOTH	We shared secretest secrets,
HE:	Those we never thought we could;
BOTH	But best we'd share, in silence,
SHE:	Our two souls in solitude.

CHORUS

HE:	Do you think we stand a chance at a second-time romance?
SHE:	Can that kind of miracle come true?
	We held tight; but we let go. Is it too late to say, "Hello?"
HE:	That's why I never said, "Goodbye." to you.
HE:	I said, "Til;" You said, "Later." 'Til' for 'til we meet again.
SHE:	We'd both be whole but not complete 'til then.
HE:	Quiet knock! A door is open; just a crack will do.
BOTH	Let's not walk away or close it. Let's walk through.'

HE:	Do you think we stand a chance at a second-time romance?
SHE:	Can that kind of miracle come true?
	We held tight; but we let go. Is it too late to say, "Hello?"
HE:	That's why I never said, "Goodbye." to you.
HE:	I said, "Til;" You said, "Later." 'Til' for 'til we meet again.
SHE:	We'd both be whole but not complete 'til then.
HE:	Quiet knock! A door is open; just a crack will do.
BOTH:	Let's not walk away or close it. Let's walk through.'

------------------------------*Present Tense*

SHE:	Did you think of me each day?
HE:	No way.
SHE:	Oh!
HE:	I'd rather not . . .
SHE:	Remember?
HE:	All the good times, yes;
BOTH:	But not what we've forgot.

(A building, increased rhythm here)

HE:	You dream of me?
SHE:	Not by a mile!
HE:	But when you did?
SHE:	It proved worthwhile.
SHE:	What have you done?
HE:	Have you had fun?
SHE:	I have a blog.
HE:	I have a dog.
SHE:	Retired?
HE:	No. just fired.
SHE:	I've become a feminist woman.
HE:	Travelled much? What did you see?
SHE:	Taj Mahal, Tipperary.
HE:	Are you married?
SHE:	He's long buried.
BOTH:	***WHAT IS IT THAT YOU REALLY WANT TO KNOW?***
HE:	Have you ever loved another more than me?
BOTH: No.	

---------------------------**R**_emembrance_

HE: To this day I can't tell you
            Why I put you on the shelf.
SHE: Other than I knew you
            Better than you ever knew yourself.
HE: Every man's a desperado
            And unable to confess
            He's not mountain-man sufficient
            And content with loneliness.
  SHE: So, if a woman needs you
           And dares to tell you so,
           Don't be lookin' for another!
           Nothing's better, little brother.
           Take her hand and follow where she goes.

CHORUS
HE: Do you think we stand a chance at a second-time romance?
SHE: Can that kind of miracle come true?
            We held tight; but we let go. Is it too late to say, "Hello?"
HE: That's why I never said, "Goodbye." to you.

HE: I said, "Til;" You said, "Later." 'Til' for 'til we meet again.
SHE: We'd both be whole but not complete 'til then.
HE: Quiet knock! A door is open; just a crack will do.
BOTH: Let's not walk away or close it. Let's walk through.

(Slow tempo with background singers. We prepare for the "sincerely" spoken chorus.)

HE: Now here's the part . . .
SHE: . . . Oh, break, my heart!
HE: Where we confess our rodeos.
SHE: Why bother? No one cares; nobody knows.
            Let's agree 'what's over's over.'
HE: You're right! When a rodeo's done
            What's left don't smell like clover

---------------------------------**Remembrance:**

BOTH: As this life goes by, there are lots of things you try,
          That next morning you wish you'd had none of;
          But there's one thing, life's golden ring, you dasn't let slip by.
          Take every chance you have to dance with love.

-------------------------------------*Present Tense*

SHE:	So, here we are.
HE:	What shall we do?
SHE:	I'm scared to death!
HE:	Take a deep breath.
SHE:	I do. I will. I did. Oh, I love you.
BOTH:	(*Asking audience*) What shall we do?
HE:	I'd rather be with you in pain
	Than ever be alone again.
SHE:	Misery is optional;
	Let's fight for happiness.
	If we think of each other first,
	Love calls that success.
BOTH:	So, here we are.
SHE:	That's true.
HE:	Because
BOTH:	I NEVER SAID GOODBYE TO YOU.

I THINK OF YOU
Robert E. McGill

CARLY: There are guys who give me *that* look every day.
KASEY: What do you? **CARLY**: I'm not curt; but I don't flirt
        I think of you. I walk away
CARLY: I bet lots of gals come on to you. **KASEY**: True.
CARLY: What do you do? **KASEY**: I tip my hat, and that is that.
CARLY: Really? **KASEY**: Always. I think of you.

CARLY: Aren't you ever tempted? **KASEY**: Well, for a moment,
        Maybe two.
CARLY: You foul, wretched cad! **KASEY**: And you?
CARLY: I wonder if a blunder would be OK with you?
KASEY: Before you stray, what do you say?
CARLY: Same thing, I hope, you do:
BOTH: I think of you.

CARLY: Suppose that I confessed to you I'd strayed.
        Heavy duty but short of all the way?
KASEY: First base, second base: OK; But third
        Or home plate? Find another place to play.
CARLY: If you strayed, I think what I would do
        Would be to slap you silly;
      (*Spoken*) Then consider how I might go about forgiving you.

    (***NOTE***: *We're taking a risk here. I expect a modern audience, especially the women, might be upset with* CARLY'S *choice. IF there is anything resembling a negative reaction, then we have an audience right where we want them. If not, then we simply need to re-write* CASEY'S *"Well, that fell flat," to "Thank you for that.")*

KASEY: WOW! That fell flat. **CARLY**: I know; but that's
        What I think love does. What about you?
KASEY: Well, I guess we all do silly things. Not ***do***!
        We ***think*** a lot of silly things, I mean.
CARLY And of all the Sillies, thinking silly things,
        You and I are the Sillies' King and Queen.

BOTH: When you love someone, you love them;
       Not always do you love the things they do;
       And you gotta ask yourself if you're the cause
       Of what you think they might have done to you.
       I guess whatever happens, first thing I should do,
       Is not think about myself but think of you.

CINDERELLA or THE BALLED SOPRANO
Robert E. McGill

With apologies to Eugene Ionesco and, YES. The correct spelling is "balled"

HE: (*As narrator*) I stopped into this single's bar I frequent every day.
A beauty, sitting all alone there, took my breath away.
I'd not seen her here before. My tongue was dragging on floor.
I was hungover from the night before; but I knew about as sure
As an almost blind drunk can assure you, I was in love at first sight.
(*Spoken*)I swore, "I'm gonna her mine, tonight."

HE: If you're alone and would enjoy some company,
I'm the same and I'd be glad to buy you . . .
SHE: . . . A cup of tea? Please don't mention alcohol
HE:, Why not?

SHE: Cinderella here's hung over, and she hasn't managed yet
   To find her way home after that damn Ball.
HE: I'll guess the princess lost more than her shoe?
SHE: Perhaps. I can't quite remember. Skip the drink.
   Buy me cigarettes; I'll tell you what I think.
HE: I'm broke, but you can bum a smoke or two.
SHE: Got a light?
HE.   Yes; and an insight: Last night I did the same as you.
Wiped out and recall only the (sordidioust, sordid-est details.)
It was an ogre's horror movie. No fairy tale.
Should we stir each other's memories? I'll try. It's up to you.

CHORUS

   Was it you or was it wasn't you
   Who danced with me last night?
   Who made love until the morning light; then vanished;
   Just disappeared completely out of sight?
   Was it you or was it wasn't you?

SHE: I remember little flashes, here and there.
HE: His winning smile? The color of his hair?
SHE: No way; he made me pay the Taxi-fare.
   I didn't care; but I thought it wasn't fair. (*She roars with laughter*)
HE*(as narrator)* She laughed at what she said interminably

HE: Whoa! That rings a bell. I'm often broke.
But I remember she laughed loud at her own jokes.
SHE: Was she smoking? **HE**: Hot? She was!
SHE: No, I mean did she like cigarettes?
HE: A lot! As I recall. She scarfed up all my smokes.

HE; Could this be true? Are you thinking what I'm thinking?
Last night, was it me and you out drinking?
SHE: (*A discovery*) A COUPLE'S OUT THERE, TWINS FOR ME AND YOU!
HE: The odds on that are pretty next to stinking.

HE: My girl, last night? You do resemble her.
SHE: You look familiar too. Could this occur?
HE: No! You said you were here in Brooklyn
I was in the Bronx.
SHE: You just *think* you were!
We're both befuddled, brain dead. Are you sure?

CHORUS

Was it you or was it wasn't you
Who danced with me last night?
Who made love until the morning light; then vanished;
Just disappeared completely out of sight?
Was it you or was it wasn't you?

HE: Well I know how to prove for sure what's true!
SHE: You mean that I was she . . ?
HE: . . That I am he, and you are you. **SHE**: How?
HE: I've got ink! A real unique tattoo! **SHE**: I've got one too!
 HE: I'll show you mine if you …
(*They are both getting ready to show their tattoos,
both of which appear to lie below the belt line on their posteriors. They
quickly re-think their plans*)

SHE: . . . until we know each other better, let it lie.
HE: It will stimulate our memories. Ink never lies.
SHE: NO! **HE**: But . . . **SHE**: Don't say butt! **HE**: But . . We might recognize
. .   **SHE**: Let's save it for later: Our fairy tale surprise.

HE: In fairy tales when lovers seek their mate,
They're ruled by magic. They must accept their fate.
I must be your prince from last night's ball.
My princess, this is our *second* date!
I've got this shoe, or this tattoo, No longer can you hide.
I've seen all and found its match. I hereby claim you as my bride.
C'mon Cinderella. My pumpkin's right outside.
By the way, my name's Sherlock Holmes. Couldn't you tell?

SHE: Thank God you're not Harry Houdini, as well.
HE: Why?
SHE: You might try to escape my lover's spell.
Let's go. (*She is laughing excessively*) Lend me a smoke.
HE: I can't, I'm broke. SHE: What's new?

BOTH: Is it you or is it isn't you?
I'M NOT LIKE YOU

Robert E. McGill

HE: A young cowpoke went drinking
At a Honky-Tonk - late night.
    SHE: A Chanteuse was singing there.
HE: He fell in love – first sight.
    SHE: But when the patrons booed her;
HE: And some rude Dude made a pass.
    SHE: Our Hero stood up for his Love.
HE: Got knocked flat on his ass.

SHE: When the fight was done, she wrapped
Her arms around his neck.
She thanked him for his bravery
And gave his cheek a peck.
HE: The stars he'd seen from punches
Sparkled in her eyes so bright.
He took her hands; knelt down and said,
"Won't you be mine tonight!"

    SHE: "Of course!" she said, "Why wouldn't I?
I've nothing else to do.
'cept I don't tumble into bed
Cuz I'm expected to.

I'm not like you. You're not like me.
Oh! By the way: One thing:
Next time you court a lady,
You'll get farther with a ring.

HE: I didn't fight so I could swipe
Your prized virginity.
 It wasn't me that hit on you.
It's them what hit on me.

A princess doesn't owe
Her hero reciprocity.
I fought defending purity.
I shed my blood for chivalry.

I'm not like you. I grant that's true
And I'm proud not to be.
I may be crude; but you're a prude.
Your kiss was like iced tea.

(Spoken) I forgot to say I love you.
I do. So, marry me!
And as for being not like me,
In matters of the heart,
We're all fruit from the same tree;
We don't fall that far apart.

        SHE: Some gals agree to be your pals.
        All the need's a shove.
        I'm something new. I won't obey
        Old rules I'm tired of.

        They'll give you ground to fool around
        For candy or a rose.
        I'll keep my sweets pure as my sheets.
        I'm holding out for love.

HE: Our realities are different,
But our truths are both the same.
Your story's not my story,
But we've both known the same pain.

If you care enough to listen
To another person's strife,
You'll learn life's not so lonely
When you dare to share a life

HER CHORUS 1

SHE: A man who's kind;
　　　　Who'll read my mind.
　　　　And when I am lost,
　　　　It's him I'll find.

　　　　He'll call me Honey; call my bluff.
　　　　Know when to hold me. When to shush!
　　　　He'll be funny; won't need money.
　　　　　　　HE: 'Til your hungry.
　　　　　　　　　SHE: *That's enough!*

HIS CHORUS 1 *and segue - with her - back to verse.*

HE: I wonder who you think you are
To set the bar so high.
Is it so that none will try
To ever get that far?
　　　　　　SHE: No. How dare you? Go!
　　　　　　Vacate this bar!

HE:　　But I'm the best
　　　　You'll ever find!
　　　　　　SHE: You're close but no cigar.
　　　　　　　Besides your blind.

SHE:　You can't see the world I dream of.
　　　　You can't see you're not for me.
　　　　　　HE:　I see how much I love you,
　　　　　　　And I'm telling you out loud.
SHE:　I'm sorry. In my world
　　　　You're not allowed.
　　　　　(A pause, as the gravity of what she's said is realized by both.)
HE:　　"I see you what you are:
　　　　You are too proud."　　　　(Shakespeare, William. TWELFTH NIGHT. Act I, scene v)

I know you'd not roll on your back
For chocolates or a rose.
Whatever led you to believe
I thought you one of those?

No, you're the kind wants fast food first;
And a movie I suppose.
A 'Chick-Flick and a Quarter Pounder
And the rounder your heels grow.

SHE: You are a horrid creature.
　　　　At Macdonald's I'll have pie.
　　　　I'll chew it up and spit it out,
　　　　And rub crust in your eye.

　　　　And for that film feature,
　　　　I'll award a generous prize
　　　　To anyone who documents
　　　　Your well-deserved demise.

HE:　They both broke out in laughter then;
　　　　SHE:　from having much fun.
　　　　　　BOTH: I think it's safe to say, "We've found
　　　　　　　　Each other's only one."
　　　　SHE:　I just wanted to make sure you were
　　　　　　As good as you seemed true.
HE:　And a guy - not like you - loves you;
　　　And he's begun to like you too.

CHAPTER 9:

COUNTRY WESTERN DRAMA & OPERA

PREFACE: A Letter from County Donegal, **1885**
Robert E. McGill

Ever since men set forth their country's flag in the conquest of hostile lands or planted their family's flag as immigrants in a friendly land, they have feared the arrival of the dreaded letter from home, announcing that their girlfriend, bride-to-be or – indeed – wife, was not prepared to wait any longer for their return. She was fiancing her affections to another. Had Penelope been less faithful to her wandering – in every sense of the word – husband, such a devastating, incoming missive might have been known as "The Dear Odysseus" letter.

However, the dubious honor of naming the despicable letter of betrayal fell to the American armed forces. During WW 11, American G.I.s pleaded with their gals at home:

> "Don't sit under the apple tree
> With anyone else but me;
> 'til I come marching home."

Those unfortunate boogie-woogie bugle boys of Company B, who found their errant Eves unable to avoid apple trees, became recipients of the infamous "Dear John" letter.

Such a fate was often shared by the lone male who ventured to a new country, scraping precious funds together to send sustenance home while also saving to bring his bride and family to the promised land. From 1850 through the early nineteen hundreds, ethnic group after group sought to position themselves inside 'The American Dream.' They established neighborhoods in large cities. Often as their people achieved true success through hard work, education and the resulting power jobs, they turned the same prejudice they had suffered on the next group of newcomers or, worse, on the poorest of their own. As the Larilie/Larilee ballad says, "Those lace curtain Irish, they won't hire their own race."

Of one thing we can be sure, the postal system thrived. Our ballad? song? one-act? – whatever this strange fish is – recounts one such exchange of lovers' letters. In this instance, they are Irish. Consequently, this is a "Dear Paidric" letter. Of course, there were Dear Ivans, Pierres, Hanses, Algernons, Abrahams: and, yes, Mohammeds, Juans and names formed by symbols. Perhaps no collection of topical literature in the world carries such diversity of origin and expression in depiction of such an indivisibly identical experience.

Do not be disturbed by the variety of rhyme schemes and the abrupt changes in verse forms. This is partially due to lack of skill and discipline; but also, it constitutes a plea for continuing collaboration by allowing the composer(s) and performers to have some "wiggle" room. Also, might it not be worth exploring the potential for changes in the standard "verse/verse/chorus" structure with various forms that tracked the changing story line and character development of the event at hand?

A LETTER FROM COUNTY DONEGAL
Robert E. McGill
NYC 1885

From Donegal to Brooklyn takes nine long days at sea;
But it seemed forever longer 'til your letter came to me.
I counted it more precious; for you must surely see
That when you do write, it's briefly and ir-reg-u-lar-i-ly
    OH, LARILEE, OH LARILIE,
      NOW, DON'T BE SHY.
    OH, LARILIE, OH LARILEE,
      SAY YOU LOVE ME?
    OH, LARILEE, OH, LARILIE, I LOVE YOU SO.
I tucked it up against my heart to shield it from the rain;
A raindrop can appear a tear; and stain sweet words with pain.
No pick-pocket – ne'er mind his strength - could pry my hands apart.
How thick it was! I thought because it held all your heart

I shed my greatcoat on the floor, I tossed my hat aside.
I kissed your note. It was your throat. Now, for what's inside
A certain call of nature, as strong as your love, called;
And, like your love, its demand was quite imperious.
Had its longings been denied, results might have proved serious.

I perched myself with dignity upon my *commode*ous throne
Your letter wasn't graced today with your unique *eau de cologne.*
No doubt, the rain, too jealous of your freshness,
Had contrived your charms be stolen.

 Just as I relieved myself of all worldly needs but you,
Dollar bills spilled out upon the floor and in my bowels, I knew.
Before reading the first line, I recalled what I had written last to you:
  I've rented a small room, more like a cupboard, but cheaper than that immigrant hotel;
  and with my raise at work our future's savings have begun to swell. I'll have enough
  to send for you come November next – FIRST WEEK! Oh, Katie, my sweet Larilee,
  we're on a streak!

    OH, LARILEE, OH LARILIE,
      NOW, DON'T BE SHY.
    OH, LARILIE, OH LARILIE,
      PLEASE SAY YOU LOVE ME?
    OH, LARILEE, OH, LARILIE, I LOVE YOU SO.

    OH, LARILEE, OH LARILIE,
      NOW, DON'T YOU CRY.
    OH, LARILIE, OH LARILIE,
      PLEASE, SHALL WE MARRY?
    OH, LARILEE, OH, LARILIE, THAT'S HOW LOVE GOES

"Dear Paidric (*not* 'Paddy' *as before.*) I'll keep this brief as there is little to tell, and I have not even the meager words to explain. However, as you see, I must, of necessity, return some of your monies.

DEAR KATIE, I know you'd always fancied being married at St. Conal's in Glenties,
Or just off the Coiste Colmcille on the banks of our Fintown's Lough Finn
But our Lady, sweet Liberty, must be your Bridesmaid here:
SAINT PATRICK'S CATHOLIC, Eleventh and Fourth Ave. Brooklyn

If the day is 'soft,' 'she'll catch a raindrop in her torch for our increase.
A Cathedral of St. Patrick's here; somewhat larger than Glenties'
but they'll have naught to do with the likes of you and I.
The "NINA" signs still grace employer's doors: "No Irish Need Apply!"

You're so industrious and so thrifty. my father wonders after Scotch in ye. Truly, Padraic, the American dollars you've sent your blessed Mother and to us are appreciated beyond even the words of our prayers; And, of course, my dear, dear and always friend, I must tell you why.

There's a park here, huge as Heaven. It's called PROSPECT: Our good luck.
It features a Zoo, a Carousel too and a lake with an island named Duck.
Within a few years your silly city fears will fade and give way
To this park's prospects; for its here that our children will play,

Shortly after you set sail a new family bought the old Curraugherty farm and began restoring it to its former glory. The family's eldest is one Timothy; and, Pat, he is a fine man. He's gentle, sweet and kind. He's not as funny as you are; but he's a good, Christian man, Padraic. He loves farming the land. He says he has no desire to see America and when I tell him of my "Big City Banshees" – as you call them - he doesn't laugh. He holds me.

Those bastard – forgive my French - lace-curtain Irish! To olde Eire they're a disgrace. They've done well themselves; Now But no matter for that fuss. I'll find a better job; and we'll be fine. There's nothing that can stop us now, so long as you are mine.

He's asked me to be his; and I've agreed. There it is. I wish you Our dear Lord's blessings on all your endeavors and I thank you for. . . I will not forget our . . . If you ever return to Eire and to Donegal, . . . well, if it be God's will, we shall meet again. Until then, although I know you must have many questions and even more to say - you are a chatterbox, my sweet - please no longer write? Let Timothy and I find our way? Please keep this last letter to remind you of me. I shall think of you on my deathbed. Good night and goodbye. Kathryn

Not a "*yours*" or an, "*I Love you*" Not even a feeble, "*fondly*" to grace a no longer familiar signature, engraved on the thin, marble headstone of this paper tomb. *"I'll think of you on my deathbed?!"* Not, *"At the moment of . . . ?"* No! Just sometime or other while I'm lying there with nothing better to do! I crumpled up the letter and hurled it at the door. It made a less than satisfactory thump and fluttered to the floor.

" Oh, Katie mine, what have you done?"
I spoke aloud as oft I did when
Reading Katie's letters;
There was so much of her in them,
From the feminine curves of her handwritten script
To the curls of her aubergine hair and her lips;
And her somewhat elegant, sensual prose.
I'd argue as if she were there.

But my Larilee's no longer here
Nor will she ever be again;
And I'm no more blind than rich.
Go bed your plowboy, Timothy,
You ignorant, sanctimonious . . . . . Witch . . . . BITCH!

I scrabbled like the creature I'd become,
But had no knowledge of.
I gathered up her letter like forgotten,
Rotten scraps of love.

Well," says I, "so much for a woman's vows and promises.
Loyalty's not what they're made of.
They're good for but an hour of the dance.
Nor are they capable of love, only romance
If you could look within their hearts?
Icy, empty caverns; hollow from the start.

By God we have New York colleen's,
The likes of which you've never seen,
who more than match your beauty,
And far outmatch your wit.

> OH, LARILEE, OH LARILIE,
>> NOW, DON'T BE SHY.
> OH, LARILIE, OH LARILEE,
>> PLEASE SAY YOU LOVE ME?
> OH, LARILEE, OH, LARILIE, I LOVE YOU SO.
>
> OH, LARILEE, OH LARILIE,
>> NOW, DON'T YOU CRY.
> OH, LARILIE, OH LARILEE,
>> PLEASE, SHALL WE MARRY?
> OH, LARILEE, OH, LARILIE
>> THAT'S HOW LOVE GOES

I thought to place your missive in a shrine that reflected its merit.
 I'd save it for all men betrayed, in order so that they might share it.
But then I thought -as is love's way -my pain too shall pass -
So, no tissue at hand, you'll understand, I used your letter to wipe my ass
And back to you may Hell's sewers bear it.
> *"Please keep this last letter to remind you of me.*
>> *Goodnight.*
>>> *Goodbye"*

> OH, LARILEE, OH, LARILIE,
> I LOVE YOU SO.
> OH, LARILEE, OH, LARILIE
> THAT'S HOW LOVE GOES

EARP AND HOLLIDAY NOTES

Robert E. McGill

COOKIE: I knew Wyatt Earp. I knew Doc Holliday as well.
Our paths crossed on the way to Hell.
Wyatt was a cruel, cold distant soul,
As we all are, so we got along quite well.

Doc was a warmer sort. He could do five things brilliantly. He made a living gambling. He knew how to love a woman, how to cook and how to drink; and he was the fastest draw the Old West ever knew.

He taught me how to do at least three of those five – I never had much luck with femininity - but I know how to cook, and drink and I know how to draw.

The trick to his draw was Doc would bend his holster leg – he was left-handed -
just a little, dropping down, as his hand lifted that pistol, so the barrel escaped the holster just a fraction of a second sooner than it might have otherwise; and he'd already filed the gunsight off the front of the gun, so that gave him another fraction of a second too.

He never aimed, he just pointed with his index finger and pulled the trigger with his middle finger; and, if Doc Holliday pointed his index finger at you, you were likely dead before you hit the ground. At least, you never knew what the Hell had happened to you until you arrived there.

There were others rumored faster than Doc Holliday; but I never saw a one could outdraw that loyal, fun-loving drunk. Never a one. The whiskey slowed the others down; or somehow impaired their skill. Whiskey oiled Doc's reflexes. The more wasted Doc was, the more likely he would kill.

Now, as for Wyatt, the reason Wyatt never took a bullet, was that Wyatt never moved. No matter if he was out in the open or how vicious the fusillade, Wyatt stood there. Wyatt just stood there, quiet and immobile as an oak.

Did you know the human eye is designed to detect movement? It will, reflexively, fly to whatever twitches inside its field of view? Go test it out. Look straight ahead, wait for a bird to fly by; and you'll be looking at it before you chose to do.

So, Wyatt stood there. Amidst the shooting and the rolling and the falling and those twirling in death's last dance, Wyatt just stood there, motionless as a tree. In all the chaos, he drew no attention; but for the motion when he finally drew his 44; and, with consummate efficiency, effortlessly and elegantly eradicated you.

If you happened to be gut shot, while you lay there, dying, crying for your mother and pleading for a drink of water, Wyatt just stood there. He had the patience of a tree. He wouldn't end your misery with a *coup de grace* to your head. Wyatt just stood there. He'd move when he was certain you were dead.

IKE AND LINDA
Robert E. McGill

THE GRISLY – BUT VERY TOUCHING - DEATH OF IKE CLANTON
at
THE O.K. CORRAL & ENVIRONS THEREBY

Wednesday, October 26th 1881, Tombstone, Arizona territory.

On one side of a narrow alley, the "Cowboy Gang" of rustlers:
Billy and Ike Clanton, Billy Claiborne, Tom and Frank McLaury.
Their names live on unto this very day. On the lawmen's side:
Virgil, Morgan and Wyatt Earp, and that hard-drinking gambler, Doc Holliday.

It was no more than nine-ten seconds that there was actual gunplay.
Seemed like ninety hours – a slow-motion commotion: Judgement Day.
In that little space of time some thirty bullets found their way
Into everyone but Wyatt. Some say Ike ran away.

He didn't! Billy Claiborne did. The following tale is what I witnessed
As the gun smoke and Ike Clanton began to fade away.
Silence sounded very loud after that furious roar
Of six-guns being fanned to fire in this little war,

Wyatt and Doc Holliday were standing,
Though the Doctor had a wound to his right arm.
Virgil and Morgan were bent over,
In pain; but breathing slow. Know why?

They were both hit bad, fair and square;
But not so bad that they were gonna die.
Doc Holliday said, "I can talk you through
What you need to do to cleanse those wounds;
And get those bullets out of you.

You're not bad off, just a little worse than I am.
Lucky those boys had lousy aim.
I've some heroin left over from my dentist days
That will alleviate the pain.

You're not yet ready for the worms.
Until then have a drink or two.
That's what I intend to do.
Lifts the spirits; kills the germs.

Remember when that Shakespeare troupe
Came through a year or two ago?
What did that actor feller say?
 "Zounds, I haveth wounds!"

I liked that play. Here we are, living it today.
Among these dead scums, some will have grieving spouses.
"Hey, Doc!" The Earps were feeling better. They were teasing.
"Would you rather be a Capulet or Montague?
Doc said. "I'm Mercutio. A plague on both your houses!'"
"Fuck all of you!"

As for Billy Clanton and the McLaury boys,
They lay face down, sprawled
In a recently created lake of blood.
You could tell by the odd angles their bodies displayed

That they were dead. Tom McLaury had but half a head.
They were among the dear who must depart;
Frank McLaury and Billy Clairborne:
Each had a couple bullets in their heart.

Wyatt tapped his boot tip up 'gainst Ike Clanton's head.
Ike was lying still; but Wyatt wanted to make sure that he was dead.
Ike's gun was nowhere to be found; Wyatt looked around.
Then he heard a wheezing, bubbling, coughing sound.

And a rapidly dying Ike Clanton said,
"Why did you have to kick me in head?
For God's sake, Wyatt, you shot me; you got me.
You've killed me, Wyatt. I'm a dying man.

I'm about to pass! What more do you want?
Show some respect! You could have kicked me in the ass.
I'm dying, Wyatt. I know it's not yet noon;
But I'll bleed out before this afternoon.

I know this is an irregular request;
However, this is somewhat of a special occasion.
You're the goddamn deputy Marshall
Can't you make a proclamation?
        Open up - and drag me into - the saloon.

Hey, Doc! Come lend a hand.
I know you can't lend two." Ike chortled.
"I winged you: you won't be prescribing meds or operating soon.
But, Doc, you sure can shoot, you drunken coot.

You could blast both eyes out of a scorpion's head,
before the God-damn bug knew he was dead."
Doc said: "Ike, don't be braggin' 'bout your shooting skills.
You really ought not to be. Only person for a couple hundred miles

Who could save your worthless life? That would be me.
But you grazed me enough so that I can't cut or sew.
I could have tended to your wounds; but you called the tune.
I'm gonna live, Ike. You're gonna die quite soon."

"C'mon Doc! C'mon Wyatt!
Drag me into that saloon.
I want to have just one more
Real good time. Send ahead for Linda!

For what she's wanted, she will surely know.
Tell her, I'd like to come before I go.
Hey! Whoa! Shit! Slow down, Fellas.
When you move too fast it hurts.

You know, Wyatt, you and I could have been pals,
Amigos. We could have lifted lots of skirts;
But you're such a gentleman I bet you flirt until it hurts.
Hang on. Let me stand up.

Let me push through those swinging doors.
I don't want to ruin my spotless reputation.
No one ever had to drag me into or out of a saloon before.
Gratias, Hombres! I hold you high in my estimation.

Let's go and get some drinks, and Linda too.
You know, you missed me, Wyatt?"
"That so?" said Wyatt, "Then where are you hit?
I don't see no bleeding. You just dying for the fun of it?"

Ike said, "You hit my gun and it exploded.
I got 30 plus little punctures in my body.
Life's passing through and out of me,
 Like light passes through a sin stained glass window.
        I'm leaving soon. Go fetch that famed ass, Linda.

Sweet Linda: smiling, drinking, eyes, all blurry.
She's usually awake by now. Tell her to hurry.

Hey, Doc! Hey, Wyatt! Could you lend a hand?
I think I'd be more comfortable on the floor.
Now, just one more chore: put a pistol in my left hand
And a card deck in my right; pour me a shot of good tequila;

And fetch my Linda to lay with me tonight.
No tears. And you guys, please, don't hover.
I need to tell my Linda girl how much I love her.
Never had the inclination. No! I never had the guts before."
Ike asked Doc, "The McCauley brothers?
"Dead." And Billy Claibourn? "Him too."
My brother, Billy? "Your brother Billy ran away."
"Son of a bitch! He's an embarrassment to the family.
          But that means more booze for Linda and we three."

Now Linda was a pavement nymph,
A ceiling gazer, a lady of the night;
But she had her standards and her sense of wrong and right.
She rushed to Ike Clanton's dying frame,

Far more true than Barbry Allen was to her dying love.
Linda was a rose and Ike Clanton was a prickly as could be.
But somehow their passion rose above
The ordinary. Memorable as foreverable,

Her name will live in Western lore,
As familiar in the memory of men
As a lass not quite as innocent as the girl next door;
But then that depends on what you're looking for.

Ike said, "I love you, Linda. Make love to me."
Now Linda was a proper girl; true to him.
She did not take his request amiss.
She bent down and sweetly, gently blew him
          A final kiss.

Linda was buried some years later
Beside Ike's grave, from which a briar grew.
In time, roses grew from Linda's grave;
And embraced Ike's briars, such was their love so true.

This was a thriller about outlaws and lawmen
Who were killers and the horrid things they had to do;
But don't forget as you pass the tale along.
It's a love story too.

Now some of you may quibble
about the authenticity of what I've told to you;
And that's alright. I welcome diversity.
Long as we don't have a gun fight,

We have a right to disagree.
So please feel free to argue with my facts.
I've added things and left things out that detract
From the way things *ought* to have been.

So, won't you all please rise above
Your obsession with what's real
And what you thought you knew?
Love is the only thing that's always true.

The End

APPENDIX: *An extra verse or two. Insert it anywhere
after Linda is on the scene, should you so desire*

Now we get to introduce a new character here

Meet one G.K., a man you'd say was all that Ike was not.
Rich and handsome, suave and hot for Linda.
He fancied he was Ike's rival. He was not.
Linda loved Ike for all his faults;

She loathed G. K.'s smarmy ways.
When he came grinning through those swingin' doors
On this one day of all, when Ike was lying, dying
On the bar room floor, Linda kicked G.K. in the balls.

Linda knew how to kick. Every whore knows that.
With her steel toed boots and pencil thin, stiletto heels,
She imagined G. K. a fine Mexican sombrero
And she tattooed him, as she would a Spanish hat.

She then returned to nursing Ike who had - as always
- something to say. "Hey, Your Lordship, Sir G. K,
Do you suppose as you're crawling out those swinging doors,
You could spare from your hair a hunk of grease

And smear it on those squeaky hinges?
Tomorrow, when you can stand up,
Come back and do the uppers.
Then every time they squeak like an emasculated mouse,
        The whole town'l think of you and cringe
        You greasy louse.

NIGHT RIDER
Robert E. McGill

The set consists of a partial representation of a small farmhouse, its back-door porch, the surrounding lawn, and a small campfire sight. Upstage, a cyclorama or projections should suggest the wide, deep fields of western Kansas and the big-skies of the frontier. The year is circa 1872. What we see of the farmhouse is the porch outside the kitchen. There is a door leading to the Kitchen. On the porch are a small table and two chairs. The furniture, like the farmhouse itself, is rustic but handsome. There should be one or two steps leading down into the yard. There should be a railing, firm enough to support an adult sitting on it, at 27." Across from the porch is a stone encircled campfire, not large but cozy. Lighting will be required to isolate the porch, the campfire, as well as areas where the Night Rider will appear.

At opening, early morning clatter of silverware on breakfast platters. At the porch table, Elizabeth, in her late 30's, a handsome widow woman, is serving breakfast to Kasey - 12 going on 18 - her only son. He is nearly finished. She is enjoying her morning coffee.

(*KASEY*)
Hey, Mom, that Night Rider man was hangin' 'round here late last night again.

(*LIZ*)
Sure you weren't dreaming, son? You oughta been asleep.

(*KASEY*)
Woke up 'round three. I really had to go. Didn't want to wake you or the baby;

(*Kasey rises and one-hand-vaults over the railing into the yard*)
So's to use the outhouse, I remembered Dad taught me how to climb out of my window. That Rider never knew from where I showed. He all but soiled his saddle. . .

(LIZ)
Kasey!
(KASEY)
Ma'am! Sorry, Ma'am. I know; but it sure was comical. If you'd been there, you couldn't helped but laugh. You'd swear his soul had left his body. The way he startled when I said, "Howdy!"
(*Liz, has finished cleaning up breakfast. Now, cup of coffee in hand, she comes down the step(s) to join Kasey in the yard. She speaks very off-handedly*)

LIZ)
Did he speak a word? Any word at all? A word for me?

(KASEY)
Momma? How did you know? He did. At least he started to; but you'll recall
That all these shenanigans got started because I had to answer Nature's call.

> *(A note here on style. This kind of moment will occur often in the play.*
> Kasey's *memory is so vivid that it creates a tangible reality. The* Night Rider
> *materializes, illuminated in his area.* Liz *sits on the porch steps, listening to*
> Kasey's *story; but not aware of the* Night Rider. Kasey *lives in "both" worlds,*
> *"telling" his story to* Liz, *while "re-living" it with the* Night Rider.)*

(KASEY)
Sir, I need to see a man about a horse, *real* bad."

(NIGHT RIDER)
Then go! Wait! This note's for Elizabeth. It's important. Something she needs to know.
I'd hoped to hand it to our Liz myself.

(KASEY)
She's not *"our"* Liz! She's *my* Mom. What's she to you? Care to explain why you've been
hanging 'round here so late and for so long?

(NIGHT RIDER)
Don't you ever sass your elders! Son. You might just lose your chance of becoming one.
You're wearing a night shirt. I'm wearing a gun. "*I-need-to-pee!*" boy hasn't one. Poor Liz.

(KASEY)
Well, I've never found it necessary to take a gun to take a whiz.

(NIGHT RIDER)
Adios, boychild! Give your limp-dick a shake for me!

(KASEY)
Vamoose! Nino Hombre! Via con el diablo!

(NIGHT RIDER)
Estupido! (*He exits; but will reappear in a "new" area)*

(KASEY)
Yeah? Well, Estupido! Too!

(LIZ)
And that was all there was to it?

(Liz *rises, steps back up onto the porch to clean up Breakfast)*

(KASEY)
He galloped off apace and stopped again, just far enough away that
If I threw a rock, I'd miss him.

(*NIGHT RIDER*)
(*In a new location*) Don't forget to pass that note along! You surely will now, won't you?

(*KASEY*)
(*Teasing*) I won't . . . forget to do so. My word's just gonna have to do. We done here?

(*NIGHT RIDER*)
Go Pee.
                    (KASEY)
I will.

(*NIGHT RIDER*)
By the time you've found relief,
I'll be long gone.

(*KASEY*)
So will my piss. Just what I'd choose.

(*NIGHT RIDER*)
What?

(KASEY)
That irritating things, Like piss and you,
Come and GO away in twos.

(LIZ)
Kasey! Where'd you learn to talk like that?

(KASEY)
Mom . . . He said the damnedest . . . *DARNDEST* thing.

(LIZ)
And what might that be?

(NIGHT RIDER)
What you want to know about who I am to your Mom and she to me, Eliza . . . Your Mom
will tell you, when she thinks you're ready. Just know this. I'm not here to do you harm.

(*KASEY*)
True?
(*NIGHT RIDER*)
"My word's just gonna have to do." Go now. Adios!

`(*KASEY*)
Hasta Luego.

(Kasey *and* Liz *are alone for the next several lines. When* Kasey *begins his
encounter with the* Rider, *we are again in a split world:* Kasey, *narrating to*
Liz *while simultaneously playing the scene with the* Rider*).*

(KASEY)
What's he up to, Momma? What's he want from us? He's out there every night. It isn't right.

(*While* Liz *wanders out into the yard, speaking as much to herself as to* Kasey,
the Rider *appears and "sets up" the Campfire environment.)*

(LIZ)
It's strange. You're right; but it's *alright*. It's what he's bound to do. He's watching out. He's
watching out for me and you.

(KASEY)
I finished with my business; thought he'd gone. When a bright, full moon pushed through the
clouds, I saw he'd spread a blanket on the lawn. He'd built a fire; unpacked his kit.

(*Here, while Liz listens <u>only</u> to Kasey, it is the Night Rider who reappears and
actually speaks the lines. Kasey either lip-syncs the speech or recites it along
with the Rider. Kasey joins the Rider at the fire. They will sit, side by side,
wrapped in the same blanket. Liz, slowly paces, behind them, listening She is
<u>only</u> aware of Kasey's narration.)*

(NIGHT RIDER)
Life's too short to waste on quarreling. You're shaking with your anger and the cold. shake
hands instead? Come on, sit down. Get warm. 'The night is long that never finds the morn.'

(KASEY)
He wrapped a wooly horse blanket 'round us; told me legends and ghost stories - some with
words we don't allow; sang songs; he cooked us up a snack. Then asked me:

(NIGHT RIDER)
You think your Dad is ever coming back?

(KASEY)
(*To Liz*) That's not his business! 'sides, who'm I to know?

(LIZ)
What did you tell him?

(KASEY)
(*To the Rider*) Honestly? I'm thinking . . . probably . . . not so. It's been – how many years
now? - seems to me - I could meet up with my own Dad and never even know. I do recall he
had this awful scar above his knee; He said it was a souvenir from a quick draw, six-gun
fight.
(*NIGHT RIDER*)
Not so! He got tossed and horn-hooked by a Texas longhorn he called *"EL MUERTE."*
 Get this! Steer's real name was "Gentle Emily."

(*KASEY*)
Did you know my Dad well?

(*NIGHT RIDER*)
Off and on. We were best friends, once, for quite a spell.

(*KASEY*)
Where is he now?
                    (*Pause.* Liz *draws nearer the fire*)

(*NIGHT RIDER*)
Not sure.

(KASEY
What was he like? I mean, like, was my father nice?

(NIGHT RIDER)
No. Couldn't say that. Sorry! You asked.

(KASEY)
It's OK. Go on.

(KNIGHT RIDER)
 Man had a jealous temper, ripe from Hell. If he got it in his head, you even looked sideways
at Elizabeth . . ? Well, Katie, bar the door! And fare, thee well! He'd call you out to shoot it
out
In what he loved to call a quick draw, six-gun fight. Nice. No. He was twice as cold as ice.
Poor Bob. He dearly loved his gun; He dearly loved his drink; and when he drank, he dearly
loved to fight. But he never learned to handle his revolver right.

            (Kasey *rises and crosses to meet* Liz *at the porch. While they speak, the* Rider
            'strikes' the campfire scene. He is preparing to leave.)

(KASEY)

(*To* Liz) He showed me his revolver; let me hold it.

(*LIZ*)

God damn!

(*KASEY*)

MAMA!

(*LIZ*)

Sorry,

(*KASEY*)

It's OK.

He made sure it was unloaded, first; fair and square. Then he showed me how to clear the barrel! Know why? He told me there were few who knew, A bullet can be *secreted* there!

(*NIGHT RIDER*)

Too many carry their guns lightly, son. A bullet's light. It doesn't make a gun weigh that much more; but a bullet *in* a gun, Gains its own eternal weight, after you've fired one.

(The Rider *exits.* Kasey *and* Liz *are back in*
REAL time: daylight, at the porch.)

(*KASEY*)

Mom read this note; he gave it to me to give to you. Said it was important. I promised him I would.

(*LIZ*)

You read it, son. Time you ought to know some . . . Read it.

(*KASEY*)

(*Reading aloud*) "My offer still stands! Now's the time." That's it? what the Hell's that mean, anyway?

(When Kasey *looks up from the note, he finds that* Liz *has run to the edge of*
their property. She has extended her arms and is circling and dipping like a
bird in flight. Kasey *chases after her. When he reaches her, she clasps him in*
a fierce embrace.)

(*KASEY*)

Why you crying, Momma? Why you dancing? Do you think, maybe it's time we go away?

(*LIZ*)
(*Taking his hands in a firm grip*) I think it's time we stay! It's time that we forgot a lot. It's
time that we forgive. Life cries out, "Love is ours to take and give." Love is all that's
necessary for the heart to live. Oh, there'll be pointing and whispering. Some always have
their two-cents worth to say. But don't think we're about to run away. What I think, Kasey –
if you agree – is that we stay.
(*She takes his hand and they walk together*)
You can't live by other people's standards. No matter what you do; they'll find a fault or two.
And given our local "other people's," standards, "Who the hell – *Pardon moi, mon
Francaise?* – would give a care to? Town folk got enough to talk about already: "Where'd
that baby come from?" I hear their whispers in my ears. Now they'll have enough gum-
flapping gossip, last them two more years. But as to how they judge me; and who I really am?
(*Spoken*) Say it with me! (*Both*) We don't give a good . . . . GOLDARN! You'll make
mistakes, my son. We all do; and when you do, Admit, atone; apologize. That part's tough.
But your forgiveness and your happiness will come riding in some late and lonely night. You
must take that love. If you have love, you have enough. Kasey, you've been my rock, my
steadfast helpmate; But you deserve a proper education. Before we lost Dad, that was our
rule. It's 'past time, darling boy, that you went back to school. I've got a man can help run
the farm. If he's not entirely a fool; knows how to use his tools. If he can plow and lift and
carry, see to my needs, he'll be more a partner than a hired and , , , , (*She sees how disturbed
Kasey has become*) Kasey, no one could ever surpass you; But at least, I'll have myself a
good right arm.

(*KASEY*)
I'm gathering you want to ask that NIGHT RIDER fella to share your life; then, second, to
come and stay - To live in here?

(*LIZ*)
He's stayed out *there* far too long. We've paid our price. We've suffered in our hunger and
our thirst.

(*KASEY*)
That means that he and you . . . ..

(*LIZ*)
Yes . .

(*KASEY*)
And he and you . .

(*LIZ*)
Yes, YES! That too. Yes, yes to everything. It was time you knew. And there's more . . .

(KASEY)
Stop! God, Mother, what more can there be?

(*LIZ*)

The worst. You need to know the worst. You need to know the worst about your Dad . . . and
me. You need to spare me your curse. Your Dad called out that man in a fit of jealousy. Kurt
– that's our late-night friend's real name – Didn't want to fight your father. They were
friends.
So, Kurt just stood there when they faced off. He didn't move. He made no move to draw.
Kurt loved us both. Killing one of us made no sense. My darling, I promised you the worst.
I swear upon my soul; your Dad drew first. Only then did Kurt draw. He killed you father
In an act of self-defense. He broke no laws. I swear, son, I'm telling you the truth. I was
there. I saw it all. . . . . I was the cause.

(*KASEY*)

So, this "fit of jealousy" had some basis in reality? Maybe a fit of adultery?

(*LIZ*)

(*Trying to slap him.*) You son of a bitch! (*He catches her wrist*))

(KASEY)

Looks like it! (*He forces her to sit on the porch stairs, hovering over her.*)
Maam, would you like to know my worst.

(*LIZ*)

Spare me your curse!

(*KASEY*)

I've done a bit of killing of my own. I told old Kurt some things I left out telling you last
night.
I hope I haven't ruined your plans.

> (*We "flash-back" to the end of the campfire scene; this time with additional
> dialogue.*)

(*KASEY*)

Then he showed me how to clear the barrel! Know why? He told me there were few who
knew,
A bullet can be *secreted* there!

(*NIGHT RIDER*)

Too many carry their guns lightly, son. A bullet's light. It doesn't make a gun weigh that
much more; but a bullet *in* a gun gains its own eternal weight, after you've fired one.

> (Liz *crosses up, as she did earlier, when this scene was first played; but turns
> back to watch the scene* Kasey *had not told her about until now.*)

(KASEY)
Mr. Night Rider Man, a word before you go? You're not as necessary as you'd like to think you are, You oughta take yourself a one-way walk. You're not needed; nor are you wanted here! I don't want to find you sneaking 'round out back. If I were you, *my Elder*, I'd just go away and stay. You might not survive another sneak attack. You're older and you're bigger; and you
Tote your *"Oh, so heavy!"* murderous gun; But I know this farm; and I'll ambush you like I did earlier today. So, ride, Night Rider! Ride! Mount up! Ride! Ride away!

> *(**Flash-back ends**. We are back, in the present. Liz and Kasey are on the porch. Neither of them has a view of the kitchen door, through which the* Night Rider *will enter momentarily. He moves behind Kasey and draws his revolver.)*

(LIZ)
No matter. You did what I'd expect you'd do, in your Daddy's place. But Son, he *will* come back. Don't you make that out to mean he's not afraid of you. He may well be; But for me and for my sake, there's no fear he wouldn't face.

> *(The* Night Rider *inserts his gun barrel into* Kasey's *ear.)*

(NIGHT RIDER)
'bout that, you best be more than crystal clear. You got a nick-name, Kasey? "THE AMBUSH KID? Don't seem so good a nick-name now, does it? Fact is things seem to have turned 'round my way.

> *(Kasey, swats the barrel of the* Night Rider's *gun away, rising rapidly.)*

(KASEY)
So, whataya gonna do, you murdering bastard? You killed my Dad. you gonna kill my whore of a mother's only son?

(NIGHT RIDER)
You talk that way again about your Mother, I'll fucking kill you.

(KASEY)
Fine! Kurt!You work on that. Right now, here's what's to be done. How 'bout, 'round seven o'clock, tomorrow morning, we draw at 30 paces? Sound fair to you?
> *(LIZ)*
Kasey, No!

(NIGHT RIDER)
Leave it, Elizabeth. There's no other way. He's as jealous crazy as his father.

(KASEY)
What's it to be, Kurt?

(*NIGHT RIDER*)

You're on.

(Kasey *has already been at the kitchen door. Now he exits rapidly.*)

(*KASEY*)

'*God e gud den,*' Everyone.

(*LIZ*)

God give you a good evening too, son.

(The **NIGHT RIDER** *stalks down the stairs into the yard. Liz follows him, throws her arms around him from behind. His anger diminishes. He turns to her; but before either can speak,* Kasey *reenters with a pistol of his own.*)

(*KASEY*)

I'll be doin' some practice shootin'. You want to cook an omelet, you gotta break some eggs; You want to kill a man, best learn to shoot a gun. What was it you said 'bout my Daddy? "He never learned to handle his revolver?" Guess you proved that true. Sorry, if you two can't get any sleep; but then I expect you'll find something to do,

(*NIGHT RIDER*)

We can do this right now if you . . . .

(*LIZ*)

Killers! You're both of you, born killers. Can't you talk of nothing else? God damn, you both! I pray Satan himself comes and takes your souls straightaway to hell. That's all that either of you is worth! Get out from underneath my roof, you fucking killers! Get off my porch, Get off my land! Get off my earth! I'm a woman; but I have done just fine all by myself; I'm a woman. I'm a human; I don't want to be all by myself. I'm a woman. Women's wombs make all the life we've got. It takes nine, long months of pain and danger doin' so. I plant life; then you take life, with a careless shot; Then you dare brag about how quickly you accomplished death. I hate you, I hate you both! Go! Go! Get out of my life. I've got better things to do than screw around with you.
(*Faint music here: the honky- tonk piano of a saloon*)
I could go into town to the saloon and sell my wares . . . I'm not that old. I could make a little money - (*Increasingly wild rage*) On the side - if I chose to lie that way; And it would be far easier than whoreing for . . . . .

(*NIGHT RIDER*)
Stand down Boy! Right now, Boy! Don't you budge! I heard you cock that pistol.
I'll let it pass this time; but I told you once before, "Don't you ever draw on me or . . .

> (*He levels his gun at* Kasey. Kasey *slowly raises his gun until it is pointed at the* Rider. *The* Rider *cocks his gun. We hear a small "pop." No one knows where it came from. The* Rider *looks surprised. He lowers his gun. He starts to cross to Elizabeth; but he can't make it. He leans against the porch fence. His gun slips from his hand. He slides to the ground.* Elizabeth *speaks in a new voice, observing, as with wonder, detached, calm, lyrical, serene.*)

(*LIZ*)
A GUN'S REPORT STARTLES THE CROWS; ECHOES BACK AND SPOOKS THEM
ONCE AGAIN. THE FARM RISES WITH THE DAWN, SILENT AS SIN.

(*KASEY*)
Mr. Kurt, he be dead, Elizabeth.

(*LIZ*)
HUSH NOW, SON. THERE'S CLEANING UP TO BE DONE. WE NEED SOME THINGS
'ROUND HERE TO DISAPPEAR. FROM THIS DAY ON, YOU'LL RUN THE FARM.

(*KASEY*)
Liz? . . . Elilzabeth?

(*LIZ*)
ELIZABETH WILL BECOME A MODEL WIDOW WOMAN.

(*KASEY*)
Mom?

(LIZ)
NO TOWN FOLK - NOT ANY MORE - DISPARAGING HER. ELIZABETH, VERY
GENTLY, ALMOST REVERENTIALLY, WITHDRAWS HER HAND FROM HER
APRON'S POCKET, REVEALING HER STILL WARM DERRINGER.

> (*Music: somber and out.*)

END

THE BALLAD OF DAFT DANNY

Robert E. McGill

VOCABULARY GUIDE:

1) "Holler" is slang for hollow, the space between two mountains.

2) *God'y'good'en!"* God, give you a good evening. A traditional Elizabethan greeting, compressed by dialect and usage

3) *Usquebah* : Pronunciation: **ew**-skah-**bah**,
   The Irish name for illegal, still-made whiskey. American variations: moonshine, white lightning, mountain dew.

4) *Cead mile failte*, pronunciation: **kade**-mee-laa-**fail**-cha.
   a hundred thousand welcomes.

THE BALLAD OF DAFT DANNY
Robert E. McGill

It is an Appalachian shindig:
    All the holler folks are here.
Daft Dan and Irish Jake fiddle melodies
    That dance away their tears.
Sunday's "Come to Meeting" services
    Are God-awful early here.
Jake wipes the rosin from his bow. It's time to go.
    The dance floor will soon clear.

Jake doesn't like to send folks home
    Without a memory.
He says, "Daft Danny, boy,
    Let's be mountain neighborly.
As they go along, sing out that song
    I taught you yesterday.
You're shy, I know; but let that go.
    Sing out generously."

So, as the elders meet up
        With their clan folk and their kin,
They say *"God'y'good'en;!"*
        And hug, until they meet again.
Young lovers steal a final kiss;
        The gossips' chatter fades,
Until Daft Danny's voice alone
        Resounds throughout the glades.

        OH, MISTRESS MINE! WHERE ARE YOU ROAMING?
        OH, STAY AND HEAR; YOUR TRUE LOVES'COMING,
        THAT CAN SING BOTH HIGH AND LOW.
        TRIP NO FURTHER, PRETTY SWEETING;
        JOURNEYS END IN LOVERS' MEETING,
        EVERY WISE MAN'S SON DOTH KNOW

Daft Danny is a wounded child;
        But from what? No one's heard.
He wandered into town one day;
        But wouldn't say a word.

"My shack's too big for me alone",
Says Jake, "Come home with me, my son."
He taught Dan how to fiddle
And to sing sweet as a bird.

Jake is an expert tinker;
        He has more than craftsmen's skill.
The metals seem to bend and soften
        To his hands and to his will.

And yet old Jake was looked upon
        With distrust and dismay until
The day he chose to lead
        The men-folk up a hill.

Hidden by his cabin was a
        Contraption he'd just built.
Drip! – Drip! – Drip! Please have a sip:
        And then have a refill.

Jake became the holler's favorite.
        He'd built a moonshine still.

Jake pretty much stays in the woods
    With Danny all the year.
At weddings, dances; living wakes
    It's their music that you'll hear.

Some dogs and little children
    Shy away from him in fear;
And no one dares to ask Jake
    Where he's from or why he's here.

Some came to flee religion;
    Some came to practice free.
Some came to hunt and work the land
    In blessed liberty.
Some heading west stopped here to rest;
    Woke up and never went away.
Some came to dig the killer coal
    And grow their family.

      They came with those possessions
      They could carry on their backs;
      But there are far more precious things
      Than those that fit in sacks.

      The soul's a roomy portmanteau
      To tote those things that count:
      Faith hope and charity and . . . oh!
      Song and dance, no doubt.
      These they carried in their hearts:
      And old Jake sought them out.
      He played their memoried melodies
      He sang their treasured words;
      And the people of the holler gladly heard.
      And Jake was here to see their music never went unheard.

        WHAT IS LOVE? 'TIS NOT HEREAFTER;
        WHAT IS LOVE? 'TIS NOT HEREAFTER;
        PRESENT MIRTH HATH PRESENT LAUGHTER;
        WHAT'S TO COME IS STILL UNSURE:
        IN DELAY THERE LIES NO PLENTY;
        THEN COME KISS ME, SWEET AND TWENTY,
        YOUTH'S A STUFF WILL NOT ENDURE.

PAOLO FAZZIOLI owns the holler's general store.
He's well to do, his house is fairly grand.
For square dances and horas, it has the biggest floor;
And Paolo has unwed daughters the male guests can't ignore.

And so, he gladly hosts this shindig weekend nights.
No drinking, politickin' mini-skirts or major fights;
When someone in the holller dies, Paolo holds a living wake;
For distant relatives have a long day's journey home to make.

Ma Fazz provides the pasta and the meats; the daughters bake.
Paolos' boys have reinforced the floor to hold the mourners' weight.
Irish Jake thanks Paolo for his hospitality.
He tells him later tonight his wife will make a plea.
    "If I were you I'd listen, and then gracefully agree."
    Paolo says, "No!" Jake clears his throat; and Paolo says, "Si, Si."

BURT OLSEN leads shy Amy out behind a nearby tree.
He aims to steal all that he can; He'll settle for a kiss.
Her father was a dead-shot sniper, Eighth Infantry.
With a shotgun at seven yards, Burt doesn't think he'll miss.

So, Burt has got a ring with him, 'case Pa gets wind of this.
Jake stops this Dad who's looking for his daughter desperately.
"Henry, you're a man of God. You'll preach to save Daft Dan? Won't you?"
So, while Henry spreads the gospel, Burt spreads his good news too.

THE TWIN VON SCHEISSBURG SISTERS
Have embraced, and not let go
Back since the gathering began
Four hours - maybe more - ago
In fact, they both came early
So they'd have privacy to speak.
They needn't fret. they *sprecht auf deutsch.*
They might as well speak Greek.

Their husbands were born brothers;
Now they're bitter enemies.
They wage a deadly feud;
Of peace they will not speak.

So, *fraulein* Helga *und ihr schweister*
This one day of the week hold hands.
They share letters, precious letters,
Words and photos from *Deutschland.*

The holler folks are generous
But what are they to do?
They do not speak the language
But there are other things to do.

The housewives would love nothing more
Than to sit and sew a quilt or make pastries;
Or they could take the sisters into town
And browse the wares at Fazzioli's'

But one husband says, "Best stay away. I'm not in the mood
To have those murderous sons of bitches perpetuate this feud.
Let the bastards kill each other off. They will not kill my brood.
The dance is fine; but that's where I draw the line. Sorry to be rude."

Jake says to Mama Fazzoli, " I bet those ladies love to shop.
They're well to do. Imagine the money they'll let drop.
Your husband brings his wares here first before they go down town.
If they can't shop there, then way not here? It would undo their frown."
          "I'll ask Paolo." says Maman; it will take a month or two.
          Old Jake winks. Mama blinks. She says, "Next Saturday will do."

PASTOR MANDERS is the Preacher Man. He leads them by example.
He announces, "Sunday service will discuss Christ in the temple."
Then he sheds his coat and tie and mingles with the crowd.
It's the home-baked pies and pastries that he's come here to sample.

Jake asks him. "Would you be so kind your social skills to share?"
I'm gonna play a square dance soon; and to complete the square
I need the widow Quinn and you to make the final pair.
"I shouldn't," says the Pastor. Jake spits twice. "But I'll be there."

PAWALSKI is the butcher, a behemoth of a man.
He can span a portly damsel's waist within his huge strong hands;
And lift her high into the sky and dance with her that way.
But there've been no damsel's in his life since his wife passed away.
          It's in her memory that he comes to shindig Saturday.

Jake speculates the man's great size is a disguise
That hides a greater heart within.
"No need to be so sad, my lad.
It's time for you to love again.
          I'll see you later on this eve;
          New lives we'll both begin."

PERE AND MAMAN DE BERGERAC
Have six and one half kids - [*spoken*: Bun in the oven.]
Folks guess a beggar's dozen is their eventual quest.
She's young enough to make it and she doesn't ever rest.

Nine months to the day that Maman last gave birth,
The midwives boil the water and sterilize the sheets.
Pere Bergerac will be anxious; and he'll smoke and have a taste
Of old Jake's *Usquebah*. "Jake, will it be alright? Can you arrange . . ?"
        Jake shrugs. He knows, in time, she'll die from this childbirth.
        Necessary providence remains beyond his skills to change.

Keeping track of six wild kids who go their separate ways,
Is what the Bergeracs accomplish every day;
But here there are many others who will watch their children prance.
Jake asks Dan to play a waltz to end the couple's day.

Dan's fiddle soars; the Bergeracs decide to share a dance.
They waltz as elegantly as a bride and bridegroom might,
Whirling in anticipation of their wedding night.
Jake is proud of Danny's music's witchery; he tells him so.

Danny is thrilled; but he asks, "Isn't it time for us to go?
Not yet, my sprite, shenanigans await the likes of you and me.
Jake whispers a suggestion in Madame de Bergerac's ear.
She says, "Non." Jake plays a note. She blushes and says, "Oui."

Maman sings like an angel, but she sings a salty song:
About a winsome holler lass.
At whom a boy from the next holler
made this holler's lass a pass.

Next time that he passed through,
She said, " It's time we wed;
For I'm already overdue."
of course, he left. she was bereft.
        She shot him in the shoe.

He got away; but to this day
- I swear this part is true –
She pines, awaiting his return,
To drop the other shoe.

PAWALSKI'S PARTNER IS MARK EPSTEIN.
"Ep" was a medic in the war.
Their dental firm serves all the nearby hollers door by door.
"We get to the problem's root!" is the motto they proclaim.
Epstein pulls the aching tooth; Pawalski pins you to the floor to ease the pain.

Old Jake corrals the two of them." I've a favor that I'd ask.
They listen but they both refuse; Jake offers them a flask.
"Those German twins are awfully shy; and don't know how to dance.
You two will swing those gals around. It's a pleasant task.".

PERE DE BERGERAC'S so busy he can't spare his spare time;
Yet his heart is filled with melody and lyrics flood his mind;
And if he could, he knows he would run off and join a band.
Meantime, he dreams his music would be of the virtuoso kind.

His one true love's the fiddle; and he dreams of what prowess -
If only he had leisure time - in time he would possess.
So, he sidles up beside old Jake, white lightning in his hand.
Downing a shot, he's got the liquid courage to profess,

"You are a man whom I respect. Your music is so fine.
Do you think - for just a moment - your fiddle could be mine?
Old Irish Jake loves nothing more than music anytime.
Bergerac's chin and Jake's violin entwine.

 "What did you say?" asks Bergerac; he heard Jake murmur low.
"Frog in my throat," Jake hands the man his bow. "He went away.
No daydreams now. *Sil vous plaît, Monsieur, Jouer.* Please play.
The hobbiless man, with trembling hand lifts a trembling bow.

The cat gut is tormented by the horse hair on its strings.
But to Bergerac's astonished ears the instrument just sings.
De Bergerac saws away, like he was cutting wood;
But the music that pours out of him's exceptionally good.
No one seems to notice this astonishing display;
And finally, gently, with a smile, Jake pries the bow away.
Next morning, when De Bergerac recalls how well he played,
He thinks it must have been a drunken escapade.

"The crazy things I get into, when I drink mountain dew."
De Bergerac never played again; nor did he wish to do.
The triumph of his one night stand served well and saw him through
The business and his lost family; for one thing he always knew:
          That someday, should he run away - he knew he never could -
          A band would hire him for sure. He just knew they would.

Daft Danny is the only one who sees and understands.
He's seen Jake many times before take matters in his hands.
When Danny's gospel lesson's finally done, he says to Jake, "Enough?"
"We're only getting started, Dan. Tonight's gonna be tough."

While these mere mortal dancers
          Waltz home to seek their sleep,
Jake tells his son they still have one
          More engagement they must keep.
For the first time Jake leads Danny
          To a hidden forest glen.
He builds a small peat fire.
          His prayers for what's to come run deep.

A motley crew appears in odd, old clothes,
          From mist wrapped wilderness.
They tune their mood with hard liquor,
          Their instruments with a caress.

"Danny, we call this whiskey "U*squebah.* "
          That means 'water of life.'
It will it bathe you in forgetfulness.
          Drink up, boys! Forget your wife!

They introduce themselves to Dan;
          And tell of their careers.
One hautboyist swears he played before
          A playwright named Shakespeare.
One fifed for George at Valley Forge
          One played taps for Abe.
Dan understands he's playing
          For our land's ancestral band.
                    (*Spoken*) And he knows fear.
Jake's rhythmic feet set forth the beat:
          And then the music soars:
Melodies and rhythms
          No one's ever heard before.
They become musical combatants,
          Each an artist warrior,
They challenge one another
          As they improvise the score.

They rest to drink and argue
            over who won the contest.
All suggest they were the best;
            But Danny's done much more.

As the dawn begins to paint
            The high peaks 'gainst the sky,
The ghostly band shakes hands with Jake;
            And say their last good-byes.
Dan asks, "Should we be going?
            We've not stayed this long before."
Saya Jake, "My Danny boy,
            I'm fine here forevermore."

The musicians eyed each other;
            Then, to Jake, they nodded heads.
One kissed Danny on both cheeks;
            And this is what he said,
'The torch has passed to you, young Dan.
            You alone can call our clan.
And always bring the Usquebah;
            It's that what binds the band."

"I'll tote you to our shack, says Dan;
            you'll catch your death outside."
Says Jake, "Tote me near the fire;
            I'm awfully cold inside."
"You daft, old 'Mick, that's just a trick
            To make me think you're dying."
"No trick, I fear." Dan sheds a tear
            "Gol-Darn, you're Irish hide!

Don't leave me, Jake. It's a mistake.
            I cannot lead the clan. Their yours."
"Don't be dafter than you have to be. Dan,"
            You make music out of madness;
            And that's all that music's for.
Here's one last song I've written for your sake.
"Cae*d mile failte*, Dan.
A hundred thousand welcomes
To each note you play, each word you sing.

May you live long, far may you roam.
Awake in every holler the music of the heart.
Meantime, I'll teach the angels country harp
To play a thousand welcomes
When you reach your final home."

Now, sing for me. I don't want to be alone.

DANNY *sings:*
All that we should aim for
     Is to do the best we can.
All that is the best in us
     Is to serve our fellow man.
All we ever really have
     Is each other every day
All we ever own
     Is the love we give away.

Reprise:
     It's an Appalachian shindig:
          Most o' the holler folks are here.

[---- end ---]

CHAPTER 10:

CODA

SLEEP WELL TONIGHT

Robert E. McGill

Lie back, sweet child. Get your Teddy Bear. Relax.
All the trains are running safely on their tracks.
 All the airplanes are haply suspended from the planets in their flight.
 No rails will crack; no harm fall from the sky tonight.

  All ships at sea – that's counting you and me –
  Will harbor peacefully beneath starlight.
  Lie back, my love. Relax! Sleep well tonight.
    THERE WILL BE OTHER TIMES TO CRY.

  Oh, yes! There will be other times to cry;
  When fame and fortune choose to pass you by;
  And the world, taking dead aim, spits in your eye;
  And you don't make it, even though you gave it your best try.
  You bet! We all get lots of other times to cry.
    Life's a song, called, "HEY, YOU!
    WHERE ARE YOU, MARCO POLO? HERE AM I."

  Life is sharing love and laughter! What else?
  After compassion, good love and better whisky,
  What will make your life complete?
  Humbly washing, as did Christ
   - without judgement - others' feet.

(*Spoken*) I believe life should be noisy. rowdy, risky!
So, go ahead and cry! But don't you ever – never. ever –
Let a moment of your precious life go by.
Cuz, it's only you that can allow yourself to live;
To humbly *take* sometimes. You don't always have to give,

  `Although, the more you give away,
  The more of you will always stay;
  Enjoy joy in tears; for tears of joy
  Will wash away all fear.

(*Spoken*) Won't you sing along to this bed-time story song?
My whole life and yours are whispering in our ears.
Lie back, my love. Hold tight; relax.
All the trains are running safely on their tracks.

146

All the airplanes are haply suspended
From the planets in their flight.
No rails will crack; no harm fall from the sky.
All ships at sea, - just like you and me – are harbored in starlight.
     Lie back. Relax! Everything's that <u>not,</u> will be all right.
     For now, let there be no longer times to cry.
        And so, Goodnight

ACKNOWLEDGEMENTS

Alan Litsey

Aldo

Carley Rose

Catherine Tambini

Connor McGill

Courtney Drumm

Daisy Nystul

Don Bristow

Dorothy Schuminski

Edmond Writers' Group

Elizabeth Rankin

Emily Haggerety

James Klagus

Janiska

John Knox

Kasey Yeargain

Kathryn McGill

Linda Borrell

Mark Johnson

Mark White

Melissa Yeargain

Patrick McGill

Ponca City Playhouse

Rick Spahr

Toni Reeder

Tony and Jan Schmitt

Tony Dobrowalski

My Special thanks and gratitude to

Frank Daley and Chyserr Nesti Monungolh for their superb guidance, honest collaboration,

editing and design skills as well as their unassailable patience.

Robert E. McGill has taught dramatic literature and directed over 100 productions in his plus fifty-year career in academic theatre. He is an award-winning poet for his translations of Greek drama.[xii] He's a buck-fifty short of being a minor Shakespearean scholar. Late in life he made the connection between today's Country Western and its origin in the music that came over to America in Shakespeare's time. He aspires to celebrating Shakespeare's curiosity and compassion for "words, words, words,"[xiii] and the human proclivity for sin and sainthood. Bob has tried to square that circle by often quoting Shakespeare. Bob also writes poetry as well as short stories, dramas and regular reproachful letters to legislators and The White House. ☺ He has kissed the Blarney Stone. More of his lyrics can be heard on the CD AND THE NIGHT GOES ON with Kasey Yeargain.[xiv]

He is married to Kathryn Huey O'Meara who is the co-founder and artistic director of OKLAHOMA SHAKESPEARE IN THE PARK, now in its thirty-fourth year under her guidance. She is a national theatrical treasure. Their eldest son, Connor, is an aspiring film author and director. Their second son, Patrick, will graduate the University of Central Oklahoma in Computer Science.

Bob believes, *"Words are birds. They sing. They soar!"* Bob holds that, *"The closer you come to the center of a system, the more its music prevails."* He believes, with his mentor, Ewald Schorm that, *"Art must be a blow to the brow and a bone in the throat."*

Professor McGill's advanced degrees are from Northwestern University and the University of Michigan. He has taught and directed at St. Lawrence University, the University of Oklahoma, Wayne State University, the University of Central Oklahoma and Oklahoma Shakespeare in the Park.

If you would like to hear more of Bob's lyrics in performance, this link will take you to the album, "AND THE NIGHT GOES ON." Kasey Yeargain composes and sings lyrics by "Emmett Mike," the stage name for: Robert Emmett Michael McGill.

https://www.kaseydillon.com/merch/the-night-goes-on-album-pre-order

---

[xii] McGill, Robert E. THE HOUSE OF THE BLIND. Sophocles' OEDIPUS REX, OEDIPUS AT COLONUS and ANTIGONE. Adapted, directed by Robert E. McGill At Wayne State Hilberry repertory Theatre. 1995
[xiii] Shakespeare, William. HAMLET. (2, 2, 192)
[xiv] THE NIGHT GOES ON. Music and Performance: Kasey Yeargain. Lyrics: Emmett Mike (Robert E. McGill) Monkey Man Studios www.kaseydillon.com